# Women
# in
# the City

## Housing, Services,
## and
## the Urban Environment

ORGANISATION FOR ECONOMIC CO-OPERATION AND DEVELOPMENT

# ORGANISATION FOR ECONOMIC CO-OPERATION AND DEVELOPMENT

Pursuant to Article 1 of the Convention signed in Paris on 14th December 1960, and which came into force on 30th September 1961, the Organisation for Economic Co-operation and Development (OECD) shall promote policies designed:

— to achieve the highest sustainable economic growth and employment and a rising standard of living in Member countries, while maintaining financial stability, and thus to contribute to the development of the world economy;

— to contribute to sound economic expansion in Member as well as non-member countries in the process of economic development; and

— to contribute to the expansion of world trade on a multilateral, non-discriminatory basis in accordance with international obligations.

The original Member countries of the OECD are Austria, Belgium, Canada, Denmark, France, Germany, Greece, Iceland, Ireland, Italy, Luxembourg, the Netherlands, Norway, Portugal, Spain, Sweden, Switzerland, Turkey, the United Kingdom and the United States. The following countries became Members subsequently through accession at the dates indicated hereafter: Japan (28th April 1964), Finland (28th January 1969), Australia (7th June 1971), New Zealand (29th May 1973) and Mexico (18th May 1994). The Commission of the European Communities takes part in the work of the OECD (Article 13 of the OECD Convention).

Publié en français sous le titre :
LES FEMMES ET LA VILLE
LOGEMENT, SERVICES ET ENVIRONNEMENT URBAIN

# FOREWORD

The OECD Conference on "Women in the City: Housing, Services and the Urban Environment" was held at OECD Headquarters in Paris on 4-6 October 1994. Over two hundred policy makers, researchers, representatives of community groups and the private sector from 27 countries as well as representatives of international organisations took part in the Conference, which was organised under the aegis of the OECD Group on Urban Affairs and the Environment Committee. Participants exchanged views and examined policies in OECD countries aimed at improving the role and contribution of women to urban development.

The publication is based upon the Issues Papers and Case Studies presented at the Conference. It includes many instructive and concrete examples of the experience and best practices in OECD Member countries aimed at improving the role and contribution of women in urban planning, the provision of housing and urban services and the improvement of the urban environment. The Conference was organised in co-operation with the Canada Mortgage and Housing Corporation and was chaired by Ms. Jean Augustine, M.P., Parliamentary Secretary to the Prime Minister of Canada.

This report, prepared by Dr. Jo Beall of the London School of Economics in collaboration with Ms. Lindsay McFarlane and Mr. Richard Ebbs of the OECD Secretariat (Urban Affairs Division, Territorial Development Service), has been submitted to the Group on Urban Affairs. It is published on the responsibility of the Secretary-General of the OECD.

# TABLE OF CONTENTS

## Chapter 1
### Opening session of the Conference

## Chapter 2
### Women in the city

## Chapter 3
### Urban policies and the planning process

## Chapter 4
## Creating liveable environments

## Chapter 5
## Urban services responsive to diverse needs

## Chapter 6
## Conclusions

## List of insets

*Chapter 1*

# OPENING SESSION OF THE CONFERENCE

## Introduction and background of the conference

In 1993, subsequent to the publication of the report on "Shaping Structural Change: the Role of Women", the Secretary-General of the OECD, Mr. Jean-Claude Paye, requested all OECD Committees to look at questions concerning the role of women in their programmes. As a result, several OECD Committees, including the Group on Urban Affairs, undertook activities which focus on raising awareness about the role of women in their policy domain. The Conference on "Women in the City", held under the aegis of the OECD Group on Urban Affairs, was part of that response.

The Conference was chaired by Ms Jean Augustine, Parliamentary Secretary to the Prime Minister of Canada. Participants included OECD Ministers and high-level, national and local government officials, representatives from research institutes and international organisations working on enhancing the role and contribution of women in urban policy making, as well as urban professionals and city and community leaders sensitive to the needs of women.

It is hoped that the Conference will contribute to understanding and promote a more general acceptance of the contribution women can make to urban development.

## *National and international fora on women, planning and the city*

The OECD Conference on "Women in the City: Housing, Services and the Urban Environment" was an important intervention on the part of the Group on Urban Affairs, given other recent activities and interventions in the urban field in relation to women and gender issues. Within OECD itself, in addition to the report, "Shaping Structural Change: the Role of Women", the OECD/DAC (Development Assistance Committee) Expert Group on Women in Development submitted to the Second DAC Meeting on Urban Development held in November 1992, a paper entitled "Integrating the Gender Variable into Urban Development".

The OECD Conference is timely in relation to other international events. Coming up shortly is the United Nations Fourth World Conference on Women: Action for Equality, Development and Peace, to be held in Beijing (China) from 4th-15th September 1995. In the past, international conferences on women have often been preoccupied with the problems of rural women. This is perhaps not surprising given that women predominate among the rural poor. However, focusing exclusively on the problems of rural women can serve to marginalise the different but legitimate needs and concerns of poor women in cities. It is hoped that this OECD report will assist Member countries to develop a gender perspective on urban issues for the Beijing agenda.

Of particular importance as well, is the forthcoming Second United Nations Conference on Human Settlements (HABITAT II) which will meet in Istanbul in June 1996. It is at this Conference that a synthesis of the conclusions and action programmes of the Rio, Cairo, Copenhagen and Beijing Conferences will be sought, in terms of their relevance for, and impact on, the urban economy and environment, and on human settlements. Much is being done by the United Nations Centre for Human Settlements (HABITAT), the Habitat Co-ordination Unit in Istanbul and National Co-ordinators, in order that a gender perspective be incorporated into Habitat II. Participating countries have been invited to include a gender perspective in all substantive issues covered by Round Table meetings and PrepCom meetings over the next two years. This report of the Group on Urban Affairs of the OECD can assist Member countries in identifying key gender issues in urban development and human settlements.

*Women, the labour market and the urban economy*

"The traditional division of work between women and men – man the bread-winner and woman the caretaker of the family – is the source of segregated labour markets, of lower income and security for women, of higher unemployment and therefore economic, financial and social dependency of women ... Individual responses to structural impediments – like part-time work in low-paid jobs, career breaks without the prospect of re-entering the labour market on adequate terms – are insufficient solutions and a waste of human potential.''

**Ms Marita Estor, Chairwoman of the OECD Working Party on the Role of Women in the Economy at OECD Conference on Women in the City, Paris, 4-6 October 1994.**

The OECD has already done significant work in the field of women and economic development, women's entrepreneurship, and women in the labour market. More recently, there has been work on women in developing countries and now, work on women and fiscal policy. However, this work has not necessarily had a specific urban focus, despite the fact that urban working women and men face particular challenges and opportunities. Hence the valuable role which can be played by the Group on Urban Affairs in bringing this perspective to bear on issues of gender and the economy.

There are two critical issues to be borne in mind when viewing the urban economy from a gender perspective. The first is **unemployment** which stands at around eight per cent in the OECD. That represents 35 million people, most of whom live in cities, and many of whom are women. For those who are employed, increasing numbers are in part-time or temporary jobs. The second issue is **globalisation** of the economy which has resulted in changing patterns of production, management, financing, technological development and information exchange. It is clear that these phenomena are gendered in their impact and that we have insufficient data and understanding of them. Furthermore, women increasingly have to work for households to survive, and they are crucial to the labour market. In some industries and in some countries, there has been a feminisation of the labour force. Moreover, male unemployment is of increasing concern in some cities, particularly among young men. It affects negatively not only their own sense of self worth and material status, but their families' well-being.

Today the spatial separation between work, community and family life is less obvious with the rise of home-work and telecommuting. At first glance this appears to offer women particular advantages, in that they are better able to combine domestic and income earning activities. Self-employment and home-working certainly appear to offer the potential for promoting business and job creation for women and men. However, it is necessary to remain alert to the potentially negative effects on women in particular and household relations in general, when private space and family relationships are utilised by employers or contractors for production.

### Women, urban social policy and physical planning

The organisation of urban areas is changing. There is a move away from planning which insists on a physical separation of functions. The era of zoning which separates home for work and leisure is being challenged. As pointed out above, changes in spatial organisation and multifunctional use of space are also entering the home-cum-office-cum-workshop. There are potential equity gains from these trends, as it is often poor communities and within them poor women, who live in marginal places and in marginal conditions. Moreover, there are potentially beneficial environmental and health spin offs from multifunctional use of space. Both traffic pollution and stress from travelling across physically and functionally segmented cities would be reduced. However, there may also be advantages to women of travelling about the city that would need to be investigated.

Furthermore, it is important that changes in the physical organisation of the city towards numerous multifunctional areas, together with the demands of city economies, do not result in a decline in urban social investment. What is required is not **less**, but **different** investment in public infrastructure, public transport, housing and urban services such as health and education. For urban social investment to be effective, it needs to be responsive to the needs of women and men in cities. For women and men to be supported as social innovators and agents of urban change, the **day-to-day** as well as the technical aspects of urban life have to be understood by policy makers and planners. Thus the facilitation of day-to-day needs should inform public expenditure, transfers and investment.

Women have very particular interests and needs in cities. In OECD countries, lone-parent families now typically comprise from 10 to 15 per cent of all families with children. Demographic trends suggest a continued rise in the numbers of lone-parents in OECD countries. The great majority of lone-parent families are headed by women (82 per cent to 91 per cent in the countries studied in the OECD report on The Evaluation of Factors Affecting the Labour Force Participation of Lone-Mothers).

More generally, social infrastructure and community services are particularly important for women in need and when well provided, the take-up is usually high. The provision of education and training services to facilitate access to employment is also critical. Women also require support services for children and elderly persons relying on them for care. Transport is another key area for women who frequently cannot afford car ownership. Women are very sensitive to the quality of the neighbourhood environment, both for themselves and because of their children. Safety both in the neighbourhood and within their own homes, is a critical issue which should be addressed in improving conditions of life for urban women and their families.

### Background of the conference

The cities of OECD countries have grown in response to the perceived spatial needs of industrialised urban economies underpinned by reliance upon ''traditional'' family structures and assumptions about gender roles. The accepted norm from the urban planning perspective was that husbands participated in paid ''production'' activities outside the home and wives took care of ''reproduction'' activities and unpaid work at home, although this organisational structure has never reflected the real life situation. The introduction of the private car; commuter-oriented public transport; zoning regulations (put in place to separate polluting industrial activities from residential areas); the quest for more affordable and more spacious housing in the suburbs; and, more recently, economic restructuring and the pursuit of economies of scale, further determined the form and structure of the central cities and suburbs we know today.

Numerous social, economic and demographic changes, as well as concern for the quality of the environment in OECD countries, are calling into question many of the basic assumptions upon which nineteenth and twentieth century urban planning has been founded. These changes relate to: the emergence of different household structures, with a decrease in the number of two-parent-and-children households; an increase in lone-parent-and-children households and persons, often elderly, living alone; the increased participation of women in the labour force; and higher unemployment of a structural nature. There is now an increased demand for more "people centred" urban policies which bring closer together the home, work and recreational facilities and which allow people living in cities to access employment and recreation and to bring up their children under better and less stressful conditions.

## *The proposal*

The proposal to hold an international conference on "Women in the City: Housing and Urban Services" was motivated by two main factors:
- The proposal responds to the request made by the Secretary-General of the OECD in 1994 inviting committees to look at the Role of Women in Shaping Structural Change.
- The proposal also responds to a need identified in the course of the Project on Housing and Social Integration based on demographic, social and economic trends in OECD Member countries. Households in need are frequently female-headed and female-headed households as a proportion of all households have been grow-ing and will probably continue to increase in OECD countries in the years to come. Policies and programmes which help these women-headed households to escape exclusion and to enter into a more stable and satisfying life-style are critical to the foundation of a healthier urban society.

"Women in the City" is not just a conference about women with problems. It is also a conference about improving the status and representation of women planners, academ-ics, policy makers, architects and community leaders. A major aim of the Conference is to accord higher visibility to women's "vision of the city" both in OECD Member countries and in the Organisation itself, in order to take more into account their views and contribution to urban society.

[Extract from Conference Proposal, October 1993]

## Opening speech by the Secretary-General of the OECD, Mr Staffan Sohlman

Madam President, Delegates, Ladies and Gentlemen,

It is a pleasure for me to welcome you to this conference on "Women in the City". I would first like to express my appreciation to Ms Jean Augustine, Parliamentary Secretary to the Prime Minister of Canada and President of the Ministerial Task Force on Social Policy Reforms, for agreeing to take on the challenging task of chairing this conference. Allow me, on behalf of the Organisation and all of us present here, to extend our warm thanks to you. I want first to explain and underline the importance which the

OECD attaches to urban questions. OECD countries are increasingly urban societies. What happens in our cities has a vital impact on economic outcomes, on social cohesiveness and on environmental development.

A dozen years go, at the initiative of Cyrus Vance, the then Secretary of State of the United States, the OECD launched a programme on urban affairs. Member countries were becoming progressively more aware that the future of their economies was intimately linked to the successful organisation of our cities. They need to be capable of both innovating and adjusting to produce new wealth, social cohesion and a better quality of life for all – for young and old, men and women alike.

Two years ago, OECD Secretary-General Jean-Claude Paye took the initiative to organise a High Level Conference to examine the range of economic, social and environmental problems of cities. This was in light of the mounting evidence which showed that the dysfunctioning of many of our urban systems threatened our capacity to grow and adjust. Further, the emergence of new forms of social inequality threatened the basis of cohesion and social harmony on which any lasting sustainable economic development could be built. That is in no way to say that we regard cities as a source of problems – more and more they represent an immense source of potential for economic growth and development. However, all of our Member countries are required to rethink the organisation of cities in such a way as to ensure that they are both cohesive and capable of change; this requires that they be capable of maximising the potential of men and women in managing the process of change. And this should be done in a way which is compatible economically, socially and environmentally. For these reasons I am delighted to welcome you here today because there is still much to be achieved in cities in relation to the needs of women and the potential of women to contribute to these common objectives.

On the economic front, it is clear that women's participation in the labour market has grown rapidly over the last 30 years. But at the same time the problems of sex discrimination and occupational segmentation remain. Nonetheless, I wish to underline the important, and in some countries, the major role that women play in the creation of new business and new employment. How our urban systems encourage women's initiative and entrepreneurship and how their particular needs are taken into account is something which all those responsible for the management of urban systems must now reflect on. For too long our gender stereotypes about who contributes to business development have tended to exclude women from playing their full role. For reasons of equity, as well as for reasons of economic and employment necessity, this should change.

So this is the first major point which I wish to underline: women have a major role to play in the economic development of our urban systems, and we need to adjust our policies and practices better to harness their talents and skills.

Cities and urban systems, like our economies, will grow in a sustainable manner only if they provide a high degree of social cohesion for all of those who live in them. The family is one of our main institutions which guarantees this stability. But we are all aware that the nature of our family structures in OECD countries has changed significantly in recent decades.

Firstly, the extended family has largely disappeared, in part because of urbanisation but also because of the way cities are organised functionally. The nuclear family has dominated the household structure for most of the past fifty years. More recently, we have seen a rapid growth of lone parent families, a factor which in itself may be neutral but we all know that lone parent families are increasingly associated with poverty and high levels of dependency on income-transfers, and that these lone parent families are often concentrated in distressed neighbourhoods.

Today, cities are increasingly faced with the problem of deprived neighbourhoods in which, for a complex of reasons, many families no longer function in a cohesive way capable of ensuring the education and transmission of values and behaviour to the young. What is clear is that until we find ways to ensure supportive family structures which are able to reinforce cultural transmission, sustain and strengthen interest in education and create families and communities with sufficient hope and opportunity to motivate our young people, we will be confronted with a problem which challenges the functioning of our societies and hence their economic prosperity.

We must now reconsider the range of policies – social, educational and housing policies in particular – which bear on the conditions necessary to create cohesive households – and this in the context of highly urban settlement patterns in OECD countries. Further, we need to examine how we can adjust our social policies so as to make them capable of providing the conditions and family environment necessary to ensure the best education of our youth. We have probably exaggerated the efficiency of measures which concentrate on social support mainly through income transfers to households. We have under-estimated the importance of investment in urban structures, housing, recreation, education, and facilities to assist in the vital process of transmission between generations. In brief, we have tended to concentrate our expenditure on consumption measures rather than on investment measures which provide opportunities for self-help and improvement. So the second point I wish to underline is that **this requires us to rethink a wide range of policies, not only urban policy per se, but also social, education and economic development policy so they become more investment-orientated: more investment in families and investment in people.**

Environmental concerns are often perceived and discussed in global or international terms: this is clearly necessary. But much can also be done at the level of their city and even the neighbourhood.

The recent conference of the Group on Urban Affairs and the Environment Committee in Heidelberg indicated the range of positive initiatives which cities are taking themselves to create a more environmentally compatible path towards development: energy conservation, access to green spaces, aesthetic beauty, public transport, exhaust fume control are all examples of ways in which cities are pioneering innovative systems to improve the environmental quality of our world.

The third point I want to underline is, therefore, that **there is a particular role for women to play in the environmental improvement of the city.** Women are often more sensitive to the quality of life which they confront on a day to day basis – for example problems of access to green space, atmospheric pollution and its effect on the health of the young. We need to see how we organise our systems of public participation in urban

15

government so as to harness the role which women can play in bringing their perception, their ideas but, over and above this, their energy and initiative to bear on finding solutions to these problems. Maybe a significantly higher proportion of women city and regional councillors would make a difference to how we deal with the urban situation.

The recent UN Conference on population in Cairo stressed the importance of education and integration of women in all aspects of our society – in the public and private sectors – as a necessary element in reducing demographic pressures and improving living conditions in developing countries. It is clear that the problems which concern our Member countries, particularly in their most distressed parts, require us to call upon the vital resources of women in solving them. If we fail to do this, we put in jeopardy the vitality and well-being of our Member countries' economies. Our objective should be to maximise the potential of women in society so that they play their full part in building a better future for all. The creativity, imagination and particular perception which women bring to bear on all of these problems has been under-appreciated in our process of policy-making.

I hope that this conference will show the way in helping to draw up a practical agenda for change in the management of our cities in order to make them more cohesive, more innovative and fairer places for all to live in. We have a collective interest and responsibility in doing this for ourselves: we have an ethical responsibility to do this for the well-being of future generations.

## Opening Address by the Chair of the Conference, Ms. Jean Augustine MP, Parliamentary Secretary to the Prime Minister of Canada

Good morning Ladies and Gentlemen.

May I say how honoured I am to be the Chair of this important international forum. We have all come here to discuss a number of critical issues related to the role of women in urban society – issues which I believe are important not just to women, but to everyone. Women's issues are ''people's'' issues. Resolving them will bring benefits to women, as well as to men and children.

This Conference provides us with an excellent opportunity to reinforce that notion and promote its acceptance among OECD countries. For my part, I am hopeful that the conference will accomplish three objectives:

- first, that it will help to increase our understanding and acceptance of the importance of gender aspects in urban development;
- second, that it will reinforce the importance of recognising gender aspects for creating gender equity; and
- third, that it will ensure that urban environments are sustainable, and respond appropriately to the needs of all residents – men, women and children.

The importance of this Conference cannot be overstated. The OECD Task Force report, Shaping Structural Change: The Role of Women, brought to our attention many significant issues relating to women in an urban context. The report pointed out the

Ms. Jean Augustine, Canada

Chair, OECD Conference
on Women in the City

inequities that currently exist in, and that are perpetuated by, a system which does not fully recognise the role and requirements of women in cities, or allow them adequate access to decision-making bodies.

We know, for instance, that the representation of women in government and industry is below that of men, so their requirements and perspectives do not receive sufficient consideration in developing urban policies and services.

Despite the fact that more women are now entering the work force, taking on the role of wage earner, either on their own or in partnership, women still carry the major burden of childcare, parent-care and homemaking. However, cities have traditionally been designed without due consideration to the particular roles women play in urban society.

The role of women in the home and community – involving mostly unpaid activities – is still undervalued. Because women are the primary caregivers and homemakers, they must leave the job market periodically in order to perform these important functions. Yet by doing so, their economic security and future job prospects suffer. This ultimately means that growing numbers of elderly women face a weak financial future or poverty.

The lack of adequate training and educational opportunities for women puts them at a disadvantage in the job market, both in obtaining and maintaining employment, as well as in seeking promotional opportunities.

Many urban services – housing, transportation, childcare, and infrastructure such as clean water, sewage, sanitation, refuse services, provision of electricity – do not adequately meet the needs of all women who are the primary homemakers and caregivers to their children and parents, or women who participate in the labour force on a part-time or non-traditional basis.

The traditional designs of cities and public transport systems pay insufficient attention to the particular activity patterns of women. The increasing insecurity in cities serves to exacerbate the isolation of women.

Urban policies in the past have created situations where women must cope with services that have not been designed and planned with their role and requirements in mind. The result: segregation, discrimination, lack of full participation in urban life, fear for personal security.

**We now recognise that urban policies must take into consideration the role and requirements of women.** We need to eliminate the many obstacles which currently exist to women's full participation in the opportunities and benefits of urban life. We need to make cities work for **all** their citizens.

It goes without saying that urban development must be more people-centred, and consider the **human dimensions** of urban living. This is, I believe, the central point which we must bring out in this Conference.

The OECD Report ''Shaping Structural Change: the Role of Women'' made several recommendations on actions to be taken to improve the role of women in cities. More importantly, the report challenged OECD countries to address these critical issues, to consider gender issues when formulating policies.

For example, we need to recognise the inter-relationship between family responsibilities and employment. We need to enhance choice and upgrading of occupations, and introduce equal pay, to eliminate occupational segregation. We need greater employment flexibility in order to meet the needs of workers. We must recognise and value diversity of lifestyles, family types and employment options, including non-market activities.

And we must create opportunities for women to participate in decision-making, either directly through representation in professions, industry and decision-making bodies, or indirectly, by being consulted before decisions affecting them are made. I am pleased that many OECD countries have taken up the challenge.

In Canada, for example, women play key roles in political, business, family and social life. They enjoy increased representation in political, business and institutional fora and they are rapidly moving out of traditionally female occupations into the professions.

Canada is also experiencing an increasing incidence of women-led households. I should state clearly that, in most cases, Canadian women have not reached equal participation. But we are moving in that direction.

We are also working to improve the situation of women in a number of areas – urban safety for instance. Initiatives are underway to make cities and neighbourhoods safer for women and children, with emphasis on transportation systems and the built environment.

Women are taking responsibility for, and control of, the provision of specialised housing such as shelters and transitional housing, as well as other forms of housing such as co-operatives, to meet women's needs.

And in the realm of human rights and the built environment, the Canadian Charter of Human Rights and Freedoms has been used to eliminate discrimination and harassment of women tenants, and to challenge exclusionary zoning practices designed to restrict the amount of special-needs housing in certain areas.

We certainly recognise that there is still much work to be done before women achieve equal participation in Canadian society. But I believe that the will exists to pursue gender issues and that we will continue to make progress towards our goal of equity.

The OECD recognises the urgency of gender issues, and the need for all OECD countries to keep the momentum going, to continue striving for progress. This conference is the expression of the movement within OECD countries to bring gender concerns to the mainstream in different policy domains and to recognise them as concerns for everyone. It is my hope that it will:

- focus our attention on further raising gender awareness in policy development;
- provide an opportunity for countries to share their experiences and successes; and
- stimulate discussions on new approaches and ideas which could be applied in our respective countries.

Our agenda reinforces the importance of these issues, and is testimony to the significant work we have ahead of us. Over the next three days we will be covering three main themes:

- The first theme – **Women and Urban Policies** – will look at women's concerns regarding how cities are planned and managed and how we can enhance their role in participating in the development of urban policies.
- The second theme – **Housing and Neighbourhood Environments Designed with Women and Children in Mind** – recognises that a critical element of the quality of life of women and children is access to affordable housing and healthy, safe home and community environments that are designed to encourage their participation, not hinder it.
- The third theme – **Urban Services Responsive to the Needs of Women and Children** – will address such issues as sharing the responsibility for child and elder-care, enhancing the mobility of women in cities, and improving education and employment opportunities for women.

The Round Table Discussions will be critical in getting all our views on the table, in focusing our attention on priority areas and reviewing the successes of OECD countries. I believe we can all learn a great deal from each other.

Our approaches might be different, but our goal is identical: to improve the role of women in determining what housing and urban services best meet the needs of **all** people regardless of gender, and how these services should be delivered.

This Conference provides an excellent opportunity to move forward in this area. But to do so, we have to be prepared to question the traditional view of gender roles, and how cities function; to look with new eyes at urban development; to recognise that family structures have changed, and that our traditional views on access to education, employment and the provision of urban services must also change. We must now work at finding creative responses to these critical issues. The OECD is well placed to make a major contribution to advancing the role of women in cities throughout the planet.

The Task Force brought the issues out some three years ago. The structural adjustment report was an excellent start. But we need to move forward, to focus our attention on critical sectors such as urban affairs and development aid, and keep the momentum going. We need to continue striving to bring progress. The OECD has a major role to play in encouraging Member countries to bring about changes and lead the way in our practices.

The issues before us are more than just areas of mutual interest. They are urgent matters which must be addressed within the context of urban planning. Resolving these issues will have a direct impact on our ability to create and foster a human dimension in our urban settings, to ensure that our cities are ''people-friendly'' and provide healthy, safe, productive environments for everyone.


**Extracts from the speech by Mrs. Françoise de Veyrinas, Member of Parliament, Deputy Mayor of Toulouse, France, Member of the National Council for Towns (Conseil national des villes)**

(Mrs. de Veyrinas was appointed Secretary of State for Deprived Urban Areas on 18 May 1995.)

Promoting the role of women in cities, helping them acquire full rights and working towards more women-friendly housing and redevelopment projects and urban services are not just a matter of ensuring parity and equality.

Because women are highly aware of human values and practicalities, and because they prefer to seek solutions not entailing power struggles, they have a different outlook on cities, on town planning and administration. Women can therefore make a special contribution to cities by bringing new dimensions to bear and restoring stability.

Women have a vital role to play in aiding urban areas, even more so than in other types of districts. Experience has shown that their active participation is always indispensable and has often been decisive in changing the situation in disadvantaged areas by, for example, restoring parental authority, strengthening social ties and getting inhabitants more involved in decisions affecting their everyday life and environment.

Several initiatives of this kind have been developed in most major French cities. Here are some examples from my own city of Toulouse.

- Family mediation procedures have been introduced in each district, using a network of mediators, most of whom are women. They aim to restore parents to their rightful place and encourage contacts between schools and mothers, who are more directly concerned by school life.
- Women living in underprivileged neighbourhoods who have succeeded socially or professionally are selected to become "solidarity links" with the aim of increasing social cohesion. These women are trained to advise local families, assist them in their dealings with authorities and help them exercise their rights.
- Women living in areas under redevelopment are encouraged, alongside all local associations, to participate in decisions affecting the urban environment. They take an active part in discussions and decision-making on the rehabilitation of housing, the reorganisation of local services and the redevelopment of communal areas.

*Chapter 2*

# WOMEN IN THE CITY

In this chapter on Women in the City, the gender dimensions of urbanisation and urban change and how these intersect with broader issues of social diversity in cities are considered. The advantages of understanding urban development in both historical and spatial terms are explored, showing why policy and planning responses need to recognise changing patterns in urban development, and the gender consequences of their impact. As these themes are explored in detail in the issue papers prepared for the conference, these are also included as part of the chapter.

## Dynamic cities: achieving sustainable change

Urbanisation is usually viewed from one of two perspectives. In the first, rural life is idealised, while urbanisation is seen as a destructive force, with negative impacts on the environment, on health and on social relations. The second view presents urbanisation as a progressive force which promotes economic development, technological innovation and socio-political sophistication. Not infrequently, women are thought to be closer to nature and the romantic rural ideal, while cities are seen as engines of growth, driven by men.

In reality, urbanisation has both positive and negative impacts on social and economic change, which involves and affects men and women alike. Cities are dynamic and present opportunities. But they can also contribute to a declining quality of life and can deny people opportunities, particularly the urban poor. The challenge facing urban policy makers and planners today is to ensure cities become and remain places where sustained social and economic development can occur, in ways which do not compromise the urban environment, or that of rural hinterlands.

For cities to plan for and manage the enormous challenges presented by urbanisation and urban growth, they need to harness the full complement of human energy available to them. This means recognising the different attributes and potential contributions of all their citizens, both women and men. However, citizenship is about rights as much as duties. Thus policy making and planning needs to take account of the diverse interests and needs of women and men, at all stages of the life cycle. Moreover, it is necessary to recognise the way in which gender intersects with other social relations such as those based on race, ethnicity and differences on the basis of income and assets.

*Urbanisation as a gendered process*

Between 1950 and 1990 the world's urban population more than trebled and by 2020 it is likely to double again. It is estimated that over 90 per cent of this increase will occur in the developing world. The urban population is growing at different rates in different regions. The industrialised nations and the countries of Latin America are the most urbanised regions, while Africa is the most rapidly urbanising continent. South and South East Asia account for one-third of the developing world's urban population and continue to experience a relatively rapid rate of urban population growth. Much of the increase in urban population can be attributed to the rapid overall growth of population in developing countries. Another contributing factor is natural increase within cities themselves. However, rural to urban migration is still a significant factor contributing to urbanisation in many developing countries.

Urbanisation is defined not only by the swelling of urban populations, but also by changes in social structures and social processes. Thus it concerns fertility and the movement of people, but it also refers to the conditions under which people in cities live. Women are traditionally targeted in policies and programmes concerned with population control or family planning. They are less often included in policies which address the growing trend towards urban work and residence.

One reason for this shortcoming may be that in many regions of the developing world, rural-urban migration has largely been a male phenomenon, particularly in South and West Asia, North Africa and the Middle East and, until recently, much of Sub-Saharan Africa. However, the urban sex ratios of most industrialised countries show the number of women to exceed that of men and the same is true for Latin America. With the exception of China where men significantly predominate, and the Philippines where women considerably outnumber men in the cities, the urban sex ratios for most of East and South East Asia are fairly balanced. Moreover, urban sex ratios are becoming more balanced in most Third World countries, partly due to the growing importance of the urban-born in accounting for urban population growth, but also because men are less commonly migrating without their families, and because it is becoming increasingly common for single women to migrate (Gilbert and Gugler, 1992).

It is significant that the greater permanence of urban populations coincides with more balanced urban sex ratios. Women play an important role as urban homemakers. Through their increased participation in the labour force and involvement in income generation, women are pivotal to the survival of urban households. They are crucial to the organisation and management of urban communities and poor neighbourhoods in particular. This role increases when cities are ill-equipped to cope with meeting the diverse needs of all urban residents.

*Gender and global trends in urban development*

With more than 75 per cent of the population of OECD countries living in cities, the Member governments of the Organisation are faced with urgent challenges caused by rapid and often unpredictable urbanisation. There is concern about urban poverty and poverty alleviation, about social conflict and cohesion, and about integrating social groups and promoting civic attitudes and action in cities. The OECD countries are also concerned about the urban environment and about how forward-looking policies can deal with present and future energy, transport and infrastructure needs, within the context of sustainable urban development. Finally, Member governments are increasingly embracing urban partnerships between the public and private sectors and community groups, as a way of working together with urban residents to resolve urban problems (MacFarlane, 1993).

Despite differences in degree, many of the problems faced by cities in industrialised countries and those in the developing world are similar. Internationally cities contribute significantly to the GDP of their countries. Yet urban productivity is often hampered by inadequate infrastructure and service support. Everywhere, the urban economy as currently constituted, fails to shorten the unemployment queues. In many cities throughout the world the informal economy is growing while production processes are changing. This process is accompanied by significant shifts in the shape and composition of the labour force. In some places there is a feminisation of labour, particularly where production is labour intensive, or in industries dependant on homeworkers.

*Urban poverty and the urban environment*

The relationship between urban poverty and the urban environment is captured in the opening line of the UNCHS (Habitat) document addressing Agenda 21 (1994). It

---

### Inset 2. **Women in cities all over the world**

I would like to underline that women in cities all over the world, in the North and in the South, often face similar obstacles, experiences and environments. The similarity of problems that women face deserves special attention during this Conference. Women in cities everywhere struggle with lack of access to housing, support services for children and elderly, education and employment, environmental protection and adequate transportation. In certain parts of the world, women are restricted in their mobility because of religious and cultural conventions such as purdah. In cities in other parts of the world, women cannot go out in the street because it is not safe: an invisible form of purdah, one might say. The rape statistics indicate that living in a city is risky for women. In several big African cities rape crisis centres have recently been set up, and exchanges are taking place between staff of these centres from different countries of the South and North. Urban and gender specialists the world over can learn from each other, and draw from each other's experiences.

*Source:* Speech by Mrs. Teresa Fogelberg, Chair of the OECD/DAC Expert Group on Women in Development (WID) to the OECD Conference on Women in the City: Housing, Services and the Urban Environment, 4-6 October, 1994.

reads, "The poorer you are, the greater the risk." Douglas (1992) says of Asian cities that "When viewing environmental distress and poverty together, the major conclusion to be drawn is that the consequences of environmental deterioration fall heaviest on the poor". In developing countries, the poor tend to locate near polluting industries, and public waste sites, and on marginal land and hazardous land. The choice of work open to them also involves them in health threatening occupations. In industrialised countries, similar patterns apply, with the urban poor clustered in high density and overcrowded housing in hazardous areas.

Cities everywhere are facing problems of urban poverty. While the plight of the homeless in the cities of Europe or North America, and that of squatters in Latin America or pavement dwellers in India cannot be compared, poverty in urban areas shares certain features. The urban poor are usually those without secure employment, savings or saleable assets, who are rendered vulnerable to changes in labour market demand, prices of basic goods, the land market and the commoditisation of housing. Women predominate among the urban poor on three counts; first, due to their location in the labour market

---

### Inset 3. **Urban poverty and the environment, Kasur, Pakistan**

Kasur is a small town in the Central Punjab in Pakistan which is rapidly industrialising by virtue of the growth of the leather industry. The poorest residents in Kasur live in the Kot Haleem settlement. Poverty in this community is characterised by high levels of male unemployment, absence of land rights and ill-health, largely as a result of occupational diseases and poor environmental conditions.

The settlement is close to the leather tanneries. Moreover, many parts of the tanning process are contracted out and are conducted from people's homes. Water in this area is badly polluted by chemical wastes from the tanneries. Sanitation conditions are poor, with no sewerage system and human excrement visible in the lanes and nearby open spaces. Open drains are blocked with heaps of solid waste.

There is visible evidence of extensive ill-health in the community, with most adults and many children suffering from chest complaints. Also reported as prevalent were eye and skin and joint problems, fever and diarrhoeal disease. High levels of heart disease, lung and breast cancer were also reported. People from the community were of the opinion that most of these diseases were caused by the widespread environmental problems and polluted drinking water.

The poorest families were those where the men had become unemployed, many through occupationally-related health problems. In these households, women were working, either in income generating activities within the household, or as domestic servants in other people's homes.

*Source:* Beall, J., *et al.*, (1993), Social Safety Nets and Social Networks: their role in poverty alleviation in Pakistan, Volume II, report for the ODA (UK) towards the World Bank Poverty Assessment for Pakistan.

which is usually in the worst paid and most insecure jobs (even where there is a feminisation of labour and high levels of male unemployment); second, due to the fact that women generally do not command equal resources or assets at the societal level; and third, due to inequities in resource distribution and decision-making power within the household (Beall, 1993).

Finally, the macroeconomic context together with the range of policy and planning responses employed to address urban poverty in industrialised and developing countries share a number of features in common. In many cities throughout the world there is evidence of "new poverty" which is predominantly an urban phenomenon and which results from the direct impact of economic reform measures. The shift towards privatisation and the inability of local authorities to deliver basic services is another shared feature of structural adjustment programmes. There is a universal shift away from transfers towards targeted safety net programmes and a multi-sectoral and integrated approach. Everywhere it is women who are increasing their labour force participation and who are picking up the burden of care, as real household incomes fall. In Europe, it is women who are being prevailed upon in the shift towards community care. In developing countries it is often women who are reducing their own consumption in the face of pressures on domestic budgets imposed by user charges or cost-sharing (Moser, 1992).

Everywhere, women are disproportionately represented among the working poor where they occupy the most poorly paid and insecure jobs. In many countries the number of women-headed urban households is on the increase, while the number of women-maintained families is also growing. The latter is the result of a growing trend in a broad range of countries, towards higher levels of male unemployment and the feminisation of the labour force.

Moreover, increased responsibility as breadwinners does not always lead to greater status or decision-making power for women. On the contrary, they often face increased conflict with unemployed husbands or partners who are unable to contribute to household income, but do not change their patterns of consumption. The global division of labour by gender is certainly not uniform, but globally, women predominate in the management of subsistence. The careful management of often scarce resources, in complicated, changing and often difficult environments, links the actions of women in cities across the world.

In many cities, populations are becoming more diverse. In some cases, diversification reflects ethnic or religious differences. In other cases the issue is one of immigration and the relations between existing urban dwellers and in-comers. In all cases, such situations pose challenges for achieving or maintaining social cohesion, particularly when different groups compete for scarce resources. It is often women, through their responsibilities in the home and their involvement with children and the neighbourhood, who play a constructive role in confronting difficulties and in keeping channels of communication open.

## Women and gender in urban research

Issues reach the policy agenda when influential groups in society identify problems, bring them to the fore and turn these into policy issues. It is not surprising, therefore, that women and gender issues were largely ignored in urban policy until they were high-lighted by feminist research and women's organisations from the 1970s onwards. Much of the impetus came from the contribution of feminist geographers and planners themselves. In addition to addressing the issue of the small number of women professionals, there was a concern to increase the quantity of material addressing gender issues and to refine the theoretical and conceptual categories of geography and planning themselves, to take into account women's interests and gender differences (see, for example, Little, Peake and Richardson, 1988). This gave rise to a number of texts which variously address the role of women in planning, the notion of planning for and with women, and the idea of gender planning (see, for example, Greed, 1994; Little, 1994; Moser, 1993; Young, 1992).

Particular areas and urban processes have been focused on defining women's position within cities, notably the way in which they use transportation, employment and housing. Such research has started with the basic assumption that women's use of cities differs from that of men. With regard to transportation, much research has documented the fact that current patterns and hours of service delivery are incompatible with the transportation needs of many women. Studies of sex segregation of the labour market and its representation across cities have shown how women are more likely than men to be located in part time work and concentrated in particular jobs in the manufacturing and service sectors. A third common field of urban research explored from a feminist perspective is housing, with much attention being paid to how the ideology of the nuclear family has impacted on housing design, thus restricting women's choice of housing options. There is also a substantial body of research on women's unequal access to housing finance.

For developing countries, the research agenda on women, gender and urban development over the past three decades is reviewed in the issue paper by Caroline Moser (see Annex 1). The paper examines the extent to which women and gender in the city has formed a separate policy research agenda, as against a part of mainstream policy research issues. In so doing it clarifies why urban gender issues have remained a marginal policy concern up to now, and identifies their critical importance for current agendas in the 1990s.


**Issue Paper: Moving towards the gendered city by Dr Jo Beall and Dr Caren Levy**


*Introduction*

Gender refers to the socially constructed roles and responsibilities of women and men and the gender relations between them in a particular historical and socio-economic context. These articulate with other social relations based on variables such as class, age, ethnicity and race. As such gender is a fundamental cross-cutting issue in the development and organisation of human settlements.

Women and men use and experience the city in different ways according to their roles and responsibilities in the gender division of labour. The gender division of labour is characterised not only by different tasks but also by their differential access to and control over resources, and the different value which is accorded to the respective activities of women and men. Gender roles and relations in urban areas are reflected in the spatial and organisational aspects of the city. This has important implications for urban policy frameworks and the ways in which cities are planned and managed.

The rapid growth of urbanisation poses an enormous challenge for human settlements development. Urbanisation is not just about numbers or the movement of people, but it is also about changes in social structures and social processes. A gender perspective shows that the urbanisation process is being accompanied by changes in gender relations at a number of different levels.

At the household level there is an increasing diversity of household types, including women-headed households, joint and extended families, and women- and/or children-maintained families. There is an important relationship between gender roles and relations, and household structure and composition. Within neighbourhoods and communities as well, gender roles and relations condition the way in which women and men engage in community management and collective action. The development of the urban economy also has a gender dimension, with women, men and children being involved in the labour force in different ways and to varying and changing degrees.

Thus urban policies, planning and management need to cater for **social diversity**, and recognise that categories currently being used in an aggregate way – such as "the household", "the community", "the neighbourhood", "the poor" – should be disaggregated on the basis of gender. Despite increasing recognition of the necessity for a gendered approach to urban development, to date this has largely been confined to a focus on "women in human settlements". This has paralleled the development of Women in Development (WID), initiated by the UN Decade (1975-85) and institutionalised over the last twenty years.

However, the institutionalisation of WID has resulted in the creation of a women's sector. This has been manifest in the emergence of WID offices in international agencies, which fund Ministries of Women's Affairs/Women's Bureaux, which in turn implement women's projects with women's groups. For a number of reasons, this sector has emerged as weak and marginalised from mainstream development activities. Intervention in human settlements development has not been immune to this process.

Building on the achievements of WID and taking up the new challenges posed by the 1990s, gender integration in urban policy, planning and management offers an alternative approach which seeks to do three things. First, it aims to increase the effectiveness of policy, planning and management by providing practitioners with the tools to integrate a gender perspective into their activities. Second, it aims to support more accountable, participatory and empowering urban development practice through a gender sensitive approach to the way in which organisations in the public, private and community sectors are constructed and interact. Finally, a gender integrated approach aims to ensure that both women and men have equal access to and control over the resources and opportunities of urban development. It is against this background that the gender dimensions of the five main themes of HABITAT II are highlighted below.

*Governance*

Neither national nor local governments on their own can meet the needs and aspirations of urban populations. Thus the balance of responsibility for urban development has begun shifting amongst the public, private and community sectors. New forms of co-operation and partnership are being attempted in an effort to muster as broad as possible a complement of material and human resources.

In this context, and often under the rubric of community participation, women are being recognised as crucial to the process of urban development. This has been largely for reasons of project effectiveness, but also derives from a genuine appreciation of their role in bottom-up local development. However, a gender responsive approach is vital to the operation of sustainable participatory urban partnerships and goes beyond merely bringing women into existing urban development priorities.

This implies two things. First, new forms of co-operation and partnership need to include both women and men from all three sectors and at all stages of policy, planning and management processes. All too often women only participate within the context of the community sector, and then only at the implementation stage. For urban development to be effective, women need to be included in decision-making as well. Second, urban development practitioners within the public, private and not-for-profit sectors need to develop gender awareness and the tools for gender competent practice, not only to achieve equity but for purposes of effectiveness.

There are a number of constraints to the development of a participatory ''tripartite'' partnership approach to urban development which also have gender dimensions. First, there seems to be a growing gap between governments and civil society. Lack of public sector transparency has encouraged political apathy and low levels of popular participation. Where government has been characterised by clientalism and patronage between the powerful and the vocal, the poor in general and women in particular have rarely benefited. Indeed, women's organisations and NGOs are often reluctant to work with public sector structures and resist ''co-option''.

Local government may be more responsive than central government to the particular needs of women and men. However, this is constrained by the fact that there is frequently political and/or financial dependence of municipal and metropolitan governments on the centre so that decentralisation is not accompanied by devolution of power.

Inasmuch as decentralisation has occurred, it has been within the public sector and has not been accompanied by a transfer of decision making functions and power between government on the one hand, and organisations of civil society on the other. This can adversely affect women and poor men, whose participation and whose interests and needs are more likely to be articulated through NGOs and community organisations than through the public sector. Participatory urban partnership requires, therefore, a commitment to gender sensitive organisational development, both in terms of intra-organisational and inter-organisational development. This is a process which is about building capacity; the capacity of women and men to be involved not just in implementation but also in the understanding and identification of problems. It involves fostering, at the metropolitan level, organisational cultures and consultational procedures, practices and processes, which are inclusive rather than exclusive of women as well as men. Failure to recognise and address the gender dimensions associated with governance and urban partnership, affects negatively on social and economic development more generally, as well as on the planning and management of sustainable human settlements.

## *Poverty reduction*

Current rates of urbanisation suggest that by the year 2000, more than half the absolute poor will be living in the cities of Africa, Asia and Latin America. Thus the burden of poverty is being borne increasingly by urban areas. And yet urban policy makers and planners are often poorly equipped to meet this challenge. A gender perspective is essential not only for understanding the characteristics and processes of urban poverty, but also to address poverty reduction sustainably and effectively. Effective urban poverty alleviation strategies are dependent on recognising that gender is a key variable in understanding and responding to the different needs of poor women and men.

Processes which promote or alleviate poverty are in operation at the macro, meso and micro levels and are gendered in their impact. At the macroeconomic level improving productivity is the primary focus of policy. Interventions of central government include investment, pricing, subsidies and credit policies. More recently they reflect ongoing structural adjustment programmes supported by the IMF and World Bank. The urban poor have been disproportionately affected by the negative impact of adjustment, such as price increases, wage restraints and reduction of subsidies on food, housing and transport.

In the face of increasing male unemployment and declining real household income and consumption, women's individual and collective coping mechanisms have become crucial to the survival of poor urban households. Increasing numbers of women are engaged in paid work, often together with their children. Women and their daughters often reduce their own consumption within households. The introduction of cost sharing for basic services has put them out of reach of the poorest, and user charges in health and education have served to increase women's caring roles within the family and to keep children, especially girls, out of school.

At the same time, structural adjustment programmes have been accompanied by "compensatory measures" or social safety nets designed to alleviate the impact of economic reform measures on the poorest. These have largely been directed at women and children, for example through supplementary feeding programmes. While poor women and children are often vulnerable and constitute an appropriate target group, such programmes fail to address the gender needs of poor men, particularly the impact of unemployment or underemployment on themselves and their households more generally.

At the micro and meso (municipal) levels poverty reduction has largely been addressed by working with or through NGOs and community organisations to support a range of activities from infrastructure upgrading through community participation, to credit programmes and micro-enterprise development. Within the context of absent or declining basic services both women and men are contributing much in the way of time and unpaid labour to their provision and maintenance in different ways. Effective urban poverty reduction strategies need to recognise the community managing roles of both women and men and the particular burden that increased community participation may place upon women in particular.

The growth of urban economies is not keeping up with accelerated urbanisation. Thus the reduction of urban poverty is increasingly being linked to the expansion of the informal sector. However, urban production and exchange today can no longer be characterised by a neat formal/informal dichotomy. Formal sector firms are becoming leaner and more flexible. They are sub-contracting parts of their operations to smaller units where fixed costs are generally lower. In the context of more flexible production processes, although men still predominate in skilled, permanent jobs in the formal sector, there are growing numbers of men among the unemployed and working poor.

At the same time, in many contexts there is an increasing proportion of women who are engaged in productive work. Women are over-represented in the non-conventional labour force and are vitally dependent on the informal economy for their own and their families economic survival. Their remuneration and returns are low, so that they too remain among the working poor. Economic and employment policy needs to recognise these gender dimensions in labour force participation.

Despite the importance accorded to the informal sector, this is rarely matched by promotional policies or by an enabling regulatory framework. To the extent that micro-enterprise development is supported, it is usually biased in favour of men, based on fairly crude gender stereotyping. Men are addressed seriously as potential small scale entrepreneurs and are provided with the necessary support to develop and expand their businesses. Women on the other hand, are encouraged, often in the context of women's groups, to engage in income generating activities with a poverty alleviation or welfare rather than a productivity bias. The underlying assumptions often are that women are secondary income earners, or that they lack entrepreneurial capacity. On this basis policies are promoted which make this a self-fulfilling prophecy. This perpetuates the existing unequal gender division of labour within the informal economy.

There is an urgent need to correct in a gender aware way, the negative regulatory and policy frameworks which currently govern the informal sector. If adequately supported by strategies to overcome constraints on their participation in productive activities, either as paid workers or independent producers, enhancing the role of women in the economy can improve women's own lives, can raise overall household incomes, and can increase aggregate urban productivity.

### Environmental management

The issue of the environment shares with gender,common experience over the last 20 years of both emerging as weak and marginal séctors in the organisation and practice of development agencies at local, national and international levels. The ineffectiveness of this sector is in part manifest in continuing urban environmental problems reflected in environmental hazards which disproportionately affect the poor and ecological deterioration of natural systems supporting the urbanisation processes. As in the case of gender, the challenge is not only to break out of the sectoral mould but to integrate the environment as a cross-cutting issue in urban development. A clearer articulation of the relation-ship between gender and the environment is also critical to the practice of a more sustainable development in human settlements. To the extent that a definition of sustain-able development encompasses socio-economic and organisational dimensions as well as a focus on the natural environment, gender, like other social relations, is important to understanding and managing human settlements in a sustainable way.

The simplest link in the gender-environment equation is the access to and control by women and men of natural resources to meet their different needs. Three issues are important here. First, it is important to recognise that there is a gender division of labour in the process of accessing resources to meet needs, reflected in the different involvement of women and men in the collection or acquisition of resources, their use, their mainte-nance and their disposal. Second, because of different gender roles, the priorities of women and men as to which gender needs will be met and when, and therefore which and when natural resources will be accessed, may differ and even conflict. Third, women and men's access to and control over resources differ by virtue of a range of social relations, including gender, class and ethnicity. In particular, poor women and men who are most disadvantaged are often exposed to the worst environmental conditions. These factors highlight the importance of disaggregating environmental problems on the basis of gender. If environmental management is to be effective, it also requires the active participation and consultation of women and men about their roles, access to and control over resources, needs and priorities.

However, to conceptualise the access to and control over resources purely in terms of women and men in households and communities, is problematic. They are not solely responsible for environmental problems. The activities in which women and men use natural resources like land, water, food, building materials and consumer goods processed from natural materials, are part of wider systems of production and consumption which are supported and maintained by economic and political interests. These systems often straddle local, national and international boundaries, and it is clear that interventions in these systems to ensure sustainable human settlement development will require the engagement of development agencies with interests at all these levels.

A key element to understanding the problem and therefore being able to formulate appropriate strategies, is to identify who is involved in the different systems of production and consumption generating and affecting urbanisation. Policy-makers and planners often make a number of stereotyped assumptions relating to gender which gives a false understanding of who is involved in particular activities.

The other central axis in the gender and environment equation is the impact of the collection or acquisition, use, maintenance and disposal of resources in systems of production and consumption at different levels. On the one hand, the impact too often takes the form of environmental hazard which is experienced differently by women, men and children in human settlements in their different roles. On the other hand, the impact is also felt on the environment. In turn, the extent to which ecological health is conserved or degraded will have implications in turn for women and men's access to resources. Thus a gendered approach to the management of the impact of environmental hazard and ecological health is also crucial, including the use of gendered indicators in monitoring.

Finally, experience from a range of countries indicates that environmental management in human settlements is being practised by a range of community level groups including women's organisations and women taking joint action with men. A gendered approach to fostering the partnership between public, private and community sectors is a key element in improving the effectiveness of environmental management in human settlements.

## *Housing*

Current debates about housing and its provision have important gender dimensions, not just in terms of their implications for women and men in communities, but also in defining successful ways of confronting problems. Two themes in these debates are particularly pertinent.

First the challenge to view housing not only as a social but also as an economic investment, highlights the necessity to recognise the different roles of women as well as men and their implications for housing provision. Under the rubric of "social development", there has been increasing recognition of the links between shelter, basic services and the reproductive role of women. Women's primary responsibility for child care and household maintenance make them a major actor at the household and neighbourhood levels. In different contexts, this has provided women with the motivation and legitimacy for taking collective action to get their needs met, for example in relation to housing, health and education. Increasingly, it has also provided an empirical rationale for development practitioners to design policies and projects to meet women's needs and to involve them in a range of ways, in interventions around housing and basic urban service provision. Within the framework of economic reform measures and privatisation, in some contexts this has extended to recognising women as being more reliable than men in cost recovery and the repayment of housing loans. Women's unpaid labour is also increasingly used along with that of men in the provision and maintenance of housing and services.

What has been less visible to practitioners is that parallel to their involvement in reproduction, many women are also contributing to household income. While in some households women may be one among many contributors, in an increasing number of households they may be sole income earners. To facilitate the balancing of their different roles, and often because of their lack of access to resources, in many contexts their economic involvement is primarily in micro-enterprises in the locality of their homes.

From the perspective of housing provision women's involvement in home and neighbourhood based production raises a number of issues. These relate to the spatial location of economic opportunities for women as well as for men at the local level. These have implications for urban economic and land use policy, planning and management. However, they also relate to the equal opportunity of women and men to use shelter itself as a factor of production, either as a place to conduct economic activity, as collateral to raise credit, or as a capital asset which can be bought and sold. In many countries, restrictive land use planning, discriminatory land tenure and legal regulations and practices are key factors which deny women the same opportunity as men to benefit from shelter as an economic investment or as a source of earning an income.

34

A second major and related theme in the current debates around housing is the promotion of enabling policies by governments, as a preferred approach to the controlling and often restrictive interventions of previous housing policies practised in many countries. An enabling approach to housing gives rise to a range of questions around the relationships between the state, communities and the private sector which have critical gender dimensions.

An important gender principle underlying enabling housing strategies should be not merely to assist women and men to perform each of their gender roles better, but to help them to combine those gender roles more easily. For example, gender responsive land use and transport policy and planning can have a positive effect in spatial, temporal and cost terms, by improving the accessibility of women and men to the different urban activities in which they engage within the existing gender division of labour.

Another crucial gender principle in enabling housing strategies is to challenge discriminatory laws and practices which deny women equal access to and control over resources, such as land and credit in many contexts. Exclusion from such resources currently prevents women's full participation in the development and benefits of housing. There is an additional danger that in the support of community self-help initiatives in housing and basic service provision, women continue to be confined to community management activities, while men dominate decision making processes.

## *Disaster mitigation, relief and reconstruction*

Urban disaster relief and disaster preparedness are becoming increasingly urgent themes in human settlements development. One reason is that the ability of many cities to physically and economically support growing populations is being put severely to the test. Material and managerial resources are being stretched by both natural and human provoked disasters, within cities and in their surrounds. These factors contribute towards heightened risks of environmental hazards and urban civil strife.

Furthermore, cities are often magnets for incomers during times of war, social conflict, or when there are natural calamities and environmental depletion in their hinterlands. Refugees, like migrants, can often find themselves in competition with each other and the local population for food, shelter, resources and employment. This can be another contributory factor to civil strife and social conflict.

Whole communities are affected by natural disasters and civil strife within urban areas. However, it is important to recognise that on the basis of their gender roles and contextually specific gender relations, women and men experience disaster and dislocation in different ways. For example, women and men face different forms of danger and risk during periods of urban unrest, rioting and civil war.

The physical and social vulnerability of women make them more likely to face extremes of deprivation and abuse in times of hardship. They are especially vulnerable to various forms of manipulation and sexual intimidation, especially when they are dependent on outside help and have to compete with others for resources. Much disaster relief is sensitive to this. However, disaster mitigation often fails to recognise two further points.

First, women are also resilient in the face of hardship and in developing countries they often play a key role in rebuilding homes, families and communities. A recognition of their role in reproduction and community management is crucial in periods of reconstruction. Women also tend to play a constructive part in mediation and reconciliation, particularly at the community level.

Second, in relation to civil strife in particular, a focus on women's vulnerability and resilience should not obscure the position of men as both victims and perpetrators of urban conflict and violence. This is clearly illustrated, for example, by the role of young men in urban gangs, who can both suffer and wreak havoc in periods of urban conflict. A gender focus is essential to more effective strategies for disaster mitigation and disaster relief.

The introduction of the concept of a relief-development continuum is useful to an understanding of disaster relief and disaster preparedness in human settlements. From a gender perspective, however, it is crucial that women are not confined to the relief end of the continuum through their being stereotyped and responded to only as victims and vulnerable groups. It is equally important that the development end of the continuum does not become the exclusive preserve of men, through similar processes of gender stereotyping. A gender approach to disaster mitigation, relief and reconstruction at the local, national and international level, would be one which provides both immediate relief and longer term opportunities to women and men alike, in full recognition of their gendered needs.

### Conclusion

The issues raised under the five themes for HABITAT II have implications for the methodologies used in policy and planning for human settlements. In conclusion, mechanisms for integrating gender into various city policy and planning processes are discussed in terms of diagnosis, consultation, organisational development and monitoring.

The way in which problems and potentials in human settlements are identified and defined, fundamentally affects strategies for urban development. If communities, target groups and households are not disaggregated on the basis of gender, then the interests and needs of women and men will not be identified or reflected in strategies for change. Thus the incorporation of gender in the way in which human settlements are conceptualised and the way in which data is collected and analysed, is a critical part of diagnosis.

Paralleling a gendered approach to diagnosis, a process of consultation which involves both women and men is a critical element for participatory urban development. Women are often excluded from the consultative and decision making processes, either by default or design. Participatory urban development, therefore, may require gender sensitive efforts and mechanisms to achieve equitable urban partnerships.

Participatory urban partnerships require a commitment to gender sensitive organisational development in the public, private and community sectors. On the one hand, this is a process of capacity building which challenges intra-organisational relations and practices in order to change organisational culture and to provide women and men with equal opportunities. On the other hand, it is a process of capacity building which demands new forms of inter-organisational, negotiation, co-ordination and delivery of urban goods and services. Urban partnerships need to facilitate the participation of representatives of weaker groups. Urban development needs to ensure equal access to and control over resources by both women and men.

Monitoring the progress of integrating gender into the Habitat II priority themes around human settlement development requires the construction of gender sensitive indicators, and the institution of gender sensitive consultation practices. The effective monitoring of conditions and performance of human settlements will undoubtedly be enhanced by this approach.

The integration of a gender approach into urban policy and the planning and management of human settlements will make urban development more effective. This is because, first, it helps ensure that targeting is appropriate to the needs of women and men respectively. Second it facilitates the active involvement of both women and men at all stages in the development process. Together these elements mitigate against project failure and the wasteful expenditure of resources and thus contribute to more sustainable human settlement development. In this sense gender is not something "extra" for practitioners to consider, but a regular part of good practice.

## Women and men in cities past and present

The issue paper by Professor Elisabeth Wilson (see this chapter below) provides an overview of culture and gender concerns in spatial development, examined from an historical perspective. Her analysis demonstrates that the design and development of cities has often been founded on very conservative images of women and their role in society.

Historically, gender has played an important and active role in the design of western cities. In other words, urban planning has not merely been gender-neutral, but has included stereotypes of gender roles and relations. In turn, urban design has become a mechanism through which gender divisions are constructed and reproduced. In the early nineteenth century, the utopian socialists and communitarians such as Charles Fourier and Robert Owen, sought to transform society by reorganising traditional domestic and community life. In both cases, although communal housework was advocated, it was still anticipated that women would carry it out.

Ebenezer Howard presented a "utopian" proposal in his "Garden Cities of Tomorrow", published in 1850. This was a precursor not only of Garden City thinking but of town planning itself. Central to his vision in the face of the overcrowded slum-ridden nineteenth century industrial city, was the Garden City as a reconciliation of city and countryside, with the union of town and country perceived as a mirror of the union of man and woman in marriage (Blake, 1994).

"The basic unit of the Garden City was to be the nuclear family. It is clear from Howard's calculations of the population, and of the workforce, that he envisaged the "male breadwinner" and "female-homemaker" household as the norm. The Garden City is designed with strict zoning separation between the location of the housing, work and leisure, thus making a rigid division between the "public" and the "private" with homemaking woman being assumed to occupy the private realm of the city. The layout of the Garden City, with its clear separation between work and the home and its single family housing let at a rent only a skilled manual worker could afford, reinforced trends of women's dependency on men and the cultivation of an ideal family of a working man, a dependent wife and child" (Blake, 1994).

The notion of an organic city was turned on its head by the influence of Le Corbusier, one of the most significant architects and urban planners of the twentieth century. Le Corbusier's "Ville Contemporaine" was ordered and each function of the city was assigned a distinct zone, linked by co-ordinated systems of transportation. Like Howard, he saw women fulfilling their "natural" role in the private sphere and favoured women's return to the home following World War I, to reduce industrial unemployment and make way for male workers. While Le Corbusier was concerned with designing a society which could balance the needs of the individual with the requirements of collective society, he based his thinking on the requirements of a standardised "modular man", whose dimensions were to be at the core of all design, from furniture to the city itself (Healey, 1994, see below).

## Issue Paper:  Culture and gender concerns in spatial development
## by Professor Elizabeth Wilson

I am most honoured to have been invited to speak at this OECD Conference. This is a very significant occasion, the first time that the Organisation has hosted a high level conference on what I believe is one of the most important, but also most neglected aspects of urban existence: what women need and want from city living, and what they can contribute.

To begin with, I want to refer briefly to two topical debates from which I believe planners and all those concerned with the development of urban life may learn something. At the recent World Conference on population, delegates were asked to consider the issue of women and to recognise that change will not take place unless women themselves are included in the planning and education processes that are intended to bring about change. Yet this recognition seemed still to be very top-down, and one of the lessons to be learned from that conference is that the empowerment of women must be an end in itself, and not merely a means to an end. The real needs of women for equality may have been hindered rather than helped by yoking it to controversial concerns open to the charge of neo-colonialism and the imposition of Western ideas. Yet, of course, women's independence is inevitably controversial, and men's interests are certainly one hidden agenda in the population debate.

The second debate is the situation of single mothers, around which controversy festers in Britain, but which I am sure is not unique to us. That some women are actually choosing to remain single because the fathers of their children can't get work and give little help in the home is actually an economically reasonable decision, and has to do more with unemployment and poverty than morals. However, there are two reactions to this: the first is when couples are exhorted to get married instead of just living together, and deplores the dependence of unmarried women on state benefits; the second is a rather crude feminist attack on young unemployed men as useless, parasitic and inherently violent. I say feminist, but although it originated from that quarter, it has been alarmingly taken up by politicians across the political spectrum. It is alarming because implicitly that argument suggests that testosterone rather than social policies determine what happens in society, and if the behaviour of these young men is held to be the result entirely of some biological imperative then that is a very pessimistic analysis, suggesting that there is nothing much we can do to restrain this biological urge.

What is only obliquely mentioned in this debate is the clear wish of women to have access to an independent source of income. The debate tends to be about the wrongness of women's financial dependence on state benefits, the implication being that they should revert to a state of financial dependence on men. But women should not be faced with the choice of financial dependence either upon the state or upon men: both are wrong and lead to distorted family relationships. The only way we can ever establish egalitarian families in which both parents have an interest in maintaining responsibility for their children is by ending the traditional division of labour whereby women cared for children and undertook a domestic servicing role towards children and husband, and men provided the family income, a fact which often prevented – and still prevents – them from undertaking the daily care of their children. Research shows that where men are involved in the daily physical and emotional care of their children they are much less likely to abuse them, and much more likely to stick by them. At present we are seeing the development of a situation that affords the worst of both worlds: women are increasingly undertaking paid employment, but usually of a part-time, casualised, badly paid type, while both unemployment and the excessively long hours some of those men who are employed are forced to work undermines the stability of relationships. What should be the focus of demands for change is the still prevalent idea that the "normal" situation is for a two parent family in which the man is the "head of the household" and the wife, at best, a so-called "junior partner" – a term many women themselves still use, by the way. For what is not recognised in these public debates is that women are voting against the unequal family system in which men wielded the power. Until we confront this issue, we can expect no improvements in social solidarity.

I have spent what may seem rather a long time on these general questions, because women's lives in the cities are dominated by them. A housing problem is always a problem about who is living in the houses. In the particular case of urban renewal and development, I hope that this conference will demonstrate not only that at last planners are willing to recognise that women must be included **from the beginning** in the decision making process if we are to be able in the twenty-first century to have cities we can live in, but also that the cities we need are cities in which women can move about freely; can find employment and can rely on safe childcare and public transport. The needs and welfare of women and children have in the past all too often been considered largely in the light of housing, thus institutionalising the patriarchal assumption that women are and should be confined to the domestic sphere. Housing is extremely important, but it is only one issue among several that must be considered.

39

It is a tragic paradox of the Western industrial period that an economic and social system which claimed to be committed to free choice, the advancement of the individual, and political equality was unable to register disadvantages of class, race and gender. Industrial capitalism never claimed that it would produce economic equality, so the presence of class differences should not surprise us, but its perpetuation of ideologies of racial and gender inferiority is rather more mysterious. Although I shall concentrate on the position of women, I shall be bearing in mind throughout that women of course do not constitute a homogenous, monolithic mass, but are also differentiated and at times divided by race, class and sexual orientation. Nonetheless, many women share a wide range of interests, aspirations and problems, and today, throughout the world, these are likely to be related to the urbanisation that has drawn so many rural dwellers to cities over the course of the past 200 years.

Ancient and outdated beliefs about women's nature and women's place persisted into the industrial period. For example, by 1900 the organised working class of largely male trade unionists was determined to emulate the bourgeois ideal of the wife and mother who remained at home and did not undertake paid employment. By no means always did ideal match reality; nonetheless that was the aspiration, albeit contested by growing numbers of middle class and working class women.

This domestic ideal originally arose with the development of what was to become a consumer society with new, higher standards of comfort and hygiene, and a changed attitude towards the upbringing of children, substituting affection for the harsh discipline of earlier times. The intensified ideal of the wife and mother in the home of course preserved men's patriarchal position at a time when the enormous economic changes that were taking place acted to erode it.

The public/private divide became more gendered than ever; woman was equated with the private sphere even in Western philosophy – it is central to the work of Hegel, for example – and, even if by default, public space became tacitly masculine. This division did not, of course, operate uniformly either within cities or across different countries, but is nevertheless crucial.

How did the – often inexplicit – assumption of gendered space influence urban planning? Not surprisingly it had enormous material effects, often very negative ones. The ideology of the public/private divide became deeply embedded in the collective unconscious.

Up until the period of the industrial revolution, cities were thought of as centres of civilisation. Already, however, with influential writers such as Jean Jacques Rousseau, there was the beginning of a romantic impulse towards the countryside, and the development of the belief that to be closer to Nature is to be closer to what is most spiritual. The view that the city is a dangerous, sinful Vanity Fair and the countryside virtuous and wholesome does not begin with the Romantics, but their development of this idea was especially powerful because cities were changing even as they wrote. In the north of England, and later all over Europe and the United States, new industrial cities filled with stench, smoke, poverty and disease. Slums sprang up and although many of the peasants and agricultural workers from the rural areas who flocked into work in the new factories saw the towns as offering a more varied and less restricted life, there was a growing distaste for the burgeoning slums and crowds, and the more people lived their lives in cities and the more distanced their lives became from their rural roots, the more desirable Nature seemed to become. Writings of all kinds, including the reports and polemical writings of a new race of philanthropists, reformers and planners all promoted and institutionalised these ideas.

The new urban world many nineteenth century writers described often seems actually hellish. Yet the nineteenth century city was also a glittering and highly sexualised spectacle. In this world, or so many felt, normal social controls and restraints no longer operated. This made the urban scene a powerful, enchanting and yet dangerous place. From this arises the nineteenth century obsession with prostitution. This obsession about prostitutes also relates to a wider and less specific fear that arose at the sight of women crowding through the streets of the new great cities; women who were not properly within patriarchal control. It was not just that the numbers of prostitutes probably increased. Rather was it not that all women who appeared unaccompanied on the streets might be prostitutes? Wasn't the woman in the street a woman of the street, a woman in public a public woman?

The woman in public even became a metaphor for a general horror of the urban crowd. Always associated with criminals, revolutionaries and minorities, the urban masses were increasingly invested with feminine characteristics, and described in feminine terms. Like women, crowds were liable to rush to extremes of emotion, and so the dangers of the crowd were the dangers of womanhood out of control.

The areas into which middle-class women might venture were very restricted. Nevertheless, the whole tendency of nineteenth century urban life was to loosen these controls. For one thing, the development of a market, consumer society provided more and more seductions for middle class women in the shape of exhibitions, department stores and refreshment rooms.

There is thus a paradox at the heart of urban life in the industrial period. Urbanisation loosened the patriarchal, familial control of women, and provided the preconditions for their greater independence. There is, indeed, research to suggest that women were freer from direct male control once they had made the journey from country to city. The bitter irony was – and still is to some extent – that the preconditions of individual rather than family based employment and the possibility of forms of relationship and household arrangements not tied to marriage and the family, were never realised. The terms upon which women entered employment in towns may have given them certain advantages by comparison with life on the farm, but they never entered employment on the same terms as men. Then, in addition, the reinforcement and institutionalisation of the domestic sphere which was an attempt to reinstate male control, and to privilege the home, was to banish, or attempt to banish women from public life.

Utopias, model villages, garden cities and town planning represented one answer to the threat of female independence. They constituted an attempt to regain control over women, although this was rarely if ever explicitly stated as a goal. They had other goals as well, of course. Utopian plans and model towns in the nineteenth century as well as promoting a more healthy environment, which was laudable, aimed to regulate the factory workers for whom they were designed more closely, to eliminate the vices of drink and promiscuous sex and to do away altogether with the urban crowd. The garden city movement was dedicated to the view that the new industrial cities were just too large, that cities should not be permitted to grow beyond a certain size, and the garden city enthusiasts were committed above all to an improvement in the domestic environment. Ebenezer Howard, the founder of the garden city movement, stated that he wished the garden cities to have the advantages of city life in terms of theatres, entertainments, museums and so on, without the disadvantages of overcrowding, slums, and long journeys to work.

You may ask what was wrong with this. The first garden city, Letchworth, in Hertfordshire, just north of London, founded in 1903, was a benign environment and in its early years attracted a bohemian community, whose members appeared very radical and included a number of independent women. Yet the movement's perfectionist attempt to eliminate all the perceived ills of big city life involved a backward looking view which idealised the village. Yet the utopianism of the scheme was at some level authoritarian and involved a clear rejection of the more riotous, violent and improper aspects of urban working class life, in which women did not behave with appropriate feminine decorum, submissiveness and modesty.

In the 1920s and 1930s, the growth of suburban life, especially in Britain and the United States, perpetuated a pale version of the garden city. Housewives, with smaller families and fewer servants, were often isolated and lonely in these new developments which usually lacked any kind of community life. Paradoxically, when architects and sociologists became critical of suburban living, they attacked it precisely because of its feminine characteristics. Yet one of the greatest modernist anti-suburbanists of the twentieth century, Le Corbusier, also defended his own approach to planning in highly gendered terms. In The Radiant City he describes an urban utopia in which married women did not and should not work. It is true that in the functional interiors he designed, much domestic labour would be done away with, replaced by a range of household gadgets, and he wished also to eliminate the stuffy overfurnished bourgeois style which itself created housework. In addition he advocated extensive public services such as communal kitchens, laundries and nurseries. The purpose of these, however, was to increase the privacy of family life by increasing the amount of time families spent on their own. The communal restaurants were to deliver food to individual households, and, above all, play schools and nurseries were not intended to free women to go to work. Their main role was to ensure eugenic standards of child care, or "scientific child rearing", and thus Le Corbusier's futuristic city was built on the most conservative of foundations: a system of rigid gender differences.

Both the garden city movement and some of Le Corbusier's ideas became widely influential after the Second World War, which inaugurated a period of rather authoritarian optimism in terms of the elimination of slums, the replanning of cities, the separation of pedestrians from traffic and so on; ideas which have more recently in their turn come under sustained attack. Such attacks often take the form of rejecting the planners who produced a synthesis of modernism and the garden city for being not just state driven but as essentially socialist. I would on the contrary argue that part of what made many such plans counterproductive was their conservatism in terms of their highly traditional view of the roles of the sexes. Most early postwar British planners at least, as well as influential writers such as Lewis Mumford, envisaged a world in which women stayed at home looking after the children and men travelled perhaps long distances to work. The attempt was to make the whole environment more domestic, and more family oriented. The pleasures of the unattached man or woman were suspect and heavily policed.

To summarise: a new anti-urban ideology developed in the nineteenth century, a central, but largely unacknowledged, aspect of which was a fear that women escaped patriarchal control in large urban centres. As a result, many of the most influential writings and much of the work of town planners acted to attempt to return women to male control in the home; their plans did not succeed in achieving that aim, but did have major and often disastrous consequences for our cities. What I am saying is that aside from the explicit and stated aims of doing away with slums, ill health and so on, there was a hidden (perhaps unconscious) agenda which was about the control of women.

Today we are living in a different time. In one sense the situation has changed: the battle to banish women from public space has been lost. In another sense women are still vulnerable, they still feel – and are – often endangered or frightened in public space and they do not in practice have the same right to walk the street that men do – even though, ironically, men are actually more likely to be attacked in public space, while women are most likely to be assaulted in the privacy of the home. In other words, women's battle for independence has neither been won nor has it been lost, and their position in society remains contested and uncertain.

Today, the demands of some campaigning women for safer streets, better public transport, public child care and the right to participate fully in the life of cities is a welcome antidote to the impulse to flee the city and create regions – as has happened most of all in the United States – that are neither city nor country, regions in which a privately owned shopping mall is the only thing even remotely resembling a public square or boulevard. For what we need is not the privatisation of urban space, housing included, but the reconquest of public space by women, men and children.

The market – shops, leisure centres, entertainment complexes (as well as state-owned museums) – has tried to bring this about to an extent, but this cannot be simply market driven. Also, the leisure industry has largely seen its enterprises in terms of that mythical entity the family: the sacred family unit with which we are becoming more and more obsessed the more it is visibly disintegrating. Neither market nor family adequately expresses what we need from our cities. We need cities in which children could once more play on their own in the street, in which women could go out with women if they so wish, in which individuals could sometimes get away from the family, in which non-kin friendship networks could form. Cities do, in fact, promote a wider variety of associations and relationships. It is this **diversity** that planners and architects in government and the public sphere must recognise as a **value**. Women do want safe streets, spaces for children to play and so on, but women need also from society the recognition that we are independent adults as well as mothers, or say, old age pensioners. The welfare model of urban development saw women largely as carers, or else perhaps more recently, as victims. Women, of course, are, and want to be mothers, want to look after their own parents and other old people, are, in some cases disabled. However, just as we want men to be involved in this world of caring and domesticity, so also do we want and need the recognition that we are also pleasure seekers and workers. Until this is recognised we shall never establish our rights to roam the city on our own terms.

## Recognising social diversity in the development of cities

That women's interests are now more effectively articulated than in the past, that their voices are increasingly being heard, and that gender issues are beginning to be addressed at the level of policy, represents one of the great successes of our era. That many women remain silent and silenced, and that a gender perspective in mainstream policy and planning is not yet an automatic part of good policy and planning practice, means that there is much work yet to be done.

The variable success of women's struggles and feminist intellectual endeavour holds two implications. First, together with those concerned with difference and discrimination on the basis of race and ethnicity, organised women have made visible at the policy level what was known at the individual level – that people are different in a variety of ways. Indeed, the recognition of social diversity and the identification of what many refer to as the post modern condition, owes much to the fields of women's and cultural studies. Second, women have the perspective, the organisational experience, and some would say the obligation, to carry forward the project of planning for diversity and difference (see issue paper by Healey, 1994 below).

Despite their lack of access to and control over resources and decision-making structures relative to men, women have greater capacity for articulating their interests and needs than say, children or the elderly. Moreover, given that women have primary responsibility for care of the old, the young, the vulnerable, sick and disabled, they may well have a vested interest in these groups being catered for and empowered by the planning process.

In recognising gender as an important variable in understanding and planning for difference and social diversity, an argument is developing that more attention needs to be paid to men's lives. In many countries there has been a decline in heavy industries where men found employment, social status and opportunities or political organisation. To the extent that new employment opportunities arise, these are often open to women rather than men. The spectre of rising unemployment promises to impact disproportionately on young men, whose response is often aggressive and violent. This is not merely a question of society now unfairly disadvantaging men rather than disadvantaging women, as was the case in the past. Rather, changing socio-economic patterns are having a profound impact on gender relations, with different consequences for women, men and children.

### Women as a Legitimate Focus of Policy

A gender perspective in policy and planning, which recognises the different interests and needs of both women and men should intersect with a perspective which is alert to

## Inset 4.  **Restructuring cities: moving to the future, Canada**

The Canadian National Report to the OECD Conference on "Women in the City: Housing Services and the Urban Environment" argues that contemporary city form is a creation of historical processes. Contemporary economics and demographics indicate a need for change. In order for cities and society to evolve, better serving the needs of all citizens, conceptualisations of cities emerging from women-centred research and from community-development approaches to urban planning need to be taken seriously. These approaches are distinct from the visions which have driven traditional urban analysis, and cities are described variously as:

- spatial expressions which are not gender-neutral but which are indicative of the relations between men and women;
- places where both women and men have other significant attributes and identities such as race, age, ethnicity and ability, which intersect with each other non-hierarchically, and which in turn influence urban spatial structures;
- places where the public and private inter-connect and where the very idea of separate public and private spheres is challenged;
- places where the majority of social services are provided by women and for women and children, and where the level of provision is closely related to women's employment;
- places where "work" needs to be defined not only as employment, but domestic and other unpaid work in the community – seen from the vantage point of the majority of women, work is a muddle of work for pay, for family and for neighbours;
- places where the content of local politics can be directed to meeting the needs of those least able to cope, and where the almost exclusive concern of local politics with production and ownership issues can be challenged;
- places where the primary instruments of urban management – planning legislation, the Official Plan, the Zoning By-law and Design Guidelines – can incorporate gender sensitivity.

*Source:* National Report, Canada, OECD Conference on Women in the City: Housing, Services and the Urban Environment, 4-6 October 1994.

other social identities and relationships such as those based on income race, ethnicity, age or ability. However, it can still be argued that women are a legitimate focus of policy in their own right.

Acknowledging women as a legitimate focus of policy is given greater justification by the fact that women are often adversely affected by the economic stringencies imposed by economic reform measures. The growing conformity around market-oriented strategies and privatisation as an instrument for improving the provision of public services at the urban level, can adversely affect women. There is a strong argument for continued state provision of some services because women have needs for services which the private sector cannot or will not meet. Those services which have built in mechanisms for generating profits will be tendered for by private firms in priority. The services with less potential for cost recovery are frequently those which address the particular gender needs of women, for example those which reduce the burden of domestic labour such as welfare assistance and child care provision (Beall, 1992).

*Women and Participatory Development*

The development of the urban economy and the urban environment cannot progress without the active participation of women. Thus women remain a legitimate focus of the policy and planning process. This aspect of "Women in the City" is explored in more detail in the following chapter. However, it is worth making reference at this point, to the OECD report "Shaping Structural Change, the Role of Women" (1991) which states:

> Decision-making systems must be responsive to change. Increased participation by a variety of actors will enhance both the effectiveness and the democratic foundations of decision-making systems. *Empowering women to participate in collective decision-making is essential for effective structural adjustment. Monitoring forms an integral part of decision-making systems.*

Decisions tend to reflect the values and perspectives of those who are involved in making them. Improving women's participation in decision making can make policies more responsive to women's needs and to the growing diversity in life and employment patterns. This means:

> "Creating an environment that encourages women to assume greater decision-making responsibilities depends on addressing the current structural barriers to involvement. That means developing positive action mechanisms to empower women and to improve their political efficacy as well as making the decision-making process more transparent and accessible." (OECD, 1991)

### Recognising children and the elderly

Cities everywhere are facing the problems posed by ageing populations. However, few cities are equipped to deal with the special needs of the elderly. As average life expectancy increases and the general health of the senior citizen improves, the number of those who need care is increasing faster than those who are able or willing to provide affordable support. Moreover, the elderly wish to remain active for as long as they can; they wish to continue working, to engage in leisure pursuits and to move about the city. And yet there are many obstacles which prevent them from easily performing daily activities in the city. A particular problem is public transport. There are also issues around urban design, for example lack of resting places and public toilets; urban services, for example garbage not being removed and therefore obstructing sidewalks.

## Inset 5.  The gentle city project, Tokyo, Japan

In Japan, the ageing society has become an issue of enormous importance. Between 1970 and 1990 the proportion of elderly (over 65 years, who are therefore predominantly female) increased from 7 to 13.5 per cent and is expected to reach 25 per cent by 2020. Japan is therefore concerned to adapt cities to meet the particular requirements of the elderly, but also of women with children and the handicapped.

In 1993 the Architects' Committee for Women of the Tokyo Society of Architects and Building Engineers participated in a study carried out in Tokyo to identify the measures necessary to create an urban environment which both improves mobility and makes travel more comfortable. The results revealed that normal, "everyday" commuting may involve a substantial expenditure of energy which is tiring even for the young, let alone for the elderly. In stations, for example, it was estimated that energy expenditures for travellers could be as high as the equivalent of walking up the stairs of a six-storey building. The timing on automatic gates and ticket-machines was found to be inconvenient for the slow or infirm. Information displays on the subway were too small for the weak-sighted elderly to read, and there was inadequate provision of ramps, escalators and places to sit and rest.

Government efforts in Japan have given rise to several projects geared towards creating a "gentle city" for the elderly and handicapped: between 1973 and 1989 the Ministry of Health and Welfare developed projects in some 300 cities and towns; the Ministry of Construction launched a "Road Construction for the Elderly" project in 1993 which aims to widen sidewalks, install pedestrian overpasses with escalators and to improve access to public transport; and in 1990 the Ministry of Transport set up a project to improve public transport for the elderly, followed in 1993 by a Traffic Planning Model for the elderly and handicapped. Another initiative by the Ministry of Construction, "Creating Space for Welfare", allows for setting priorities, identifying goals and drawing up guidelines focused on the requirements of the elderly, the handicapped and women with children.

*Source:* Matsukawa, J. (1994) "Tokyo Travel: Urban Space to Move Around Tokyo", paper presented to the OECD Conference on Women in the City: Housing, Services and the Urban Environment, 4-6 October 1994.

---

The elderly also have special concerns and needs in relation to housing and the lived environment. Elderly women are particularly vulnerable to crime and violence, and disadvantaged by residential locations far from shops and services such as clinics and libraries. The issue of the housing needs of the elderly, the vast majority of whom are women in single headed households, are covered in chapter four below.

According to UNICEF, nearly half of the global urban population are children. Moreover, where available, disaggregated data suggests that urban children fare worse than the national average in many countries and they are often worse off than their rural counterparts. Children are being adversely affected by a number of socio-economic changes, particularly a combination of increased labour force participation by women in low-paid, informal jobs, and increasing male unemployment. The high proportion of lone parent families, usually headed by a mother, are well represented among the urban poor, and children in these households are vulnerable as a result of social deprivation. Globally, poverty is responsible for producing more working and street children and for increasing the incidence of child abuse and abandonment. The growing phenomenon of urban ''street'' children – either unaccompanied by adults or, more commonly, living with their families by night and working the streets by day – is also associated with family breakdown (Boyden, 1991).

However, children are not only an urban problem but an urban resource. Cities of the developing world have predominantly youthful populations. Children represent human capital and are worthy of social investment. They are also capable of enriching the content of urban policy and planning, if appropriately consulted with respect to their schools and neighbourhoods (see Inset 7).

## Culture and ethnicity in cities and towns

Cities have heterogeneous populations comprising long-standing urban residents, rural migrants and refugees with different racial, ethnic, cultural, religious and linguistic origins. Social diversity based on these variables as well as those of income, age and gender, is likely to create new tensions, particularly when people from different backgrounds are forced to live together in overcrowded conditions and have to compete for scarce resources. People develop their own individual and collective survival strategies.

48

## Inset 7.  The child-planners of Kitee, Finland

Kitee is a small rural town in north eastern Finland. In a "problem neighbourhood" of 2000 residents, it was decided that children might participate in its improvement. In 1992 a special teacher-led club was formed and met twice a week after school. The project was supported by the Ministry of the Environment and that of Health and Social Affairs. An architect and environmental psychologist were hired to animate the planning and evaluate the project.

Through various participatory techniques, children and residents helped to formulate goals, using visual methods such as drawing, writing, photography and model building. The issue of traffic safety in the area was taken up and was turned into an official citizen initiative for which public funds were allocated. On the whole, however, the project is largely at the problem identification and needs assessment stage, and there is a search for new solutions and ways of translating them into praxis. This will take some time.

However, the project has shown children to be surprisingly good urban planners. They demonstrated a good conception of scale, and paid greater attention to detail than an architect previously hired to renovate the school before the Kitee project started. What their approach revealed was the need to facilitate diverse types of encounters and exchanges between children themselves and between children and adults.

Perhaps the most surprising result of the children's neighbourhood planning was their ability to deal with the residential areas as a whole. The children's contribution has put pressure on the town to expand the content of urban planning to cover ecological and social issues. There is demand for the planning process to include groups like children, young people, the elderly and women.

*Source:* Horelli, L. (1994), "Children as a Resource in Urban Policy, Experiences from Kitee, Finland", paper presented to the OECD Conference, Women in the City: Housing, Services and the Urban Environment, 4-6 October 1994.

Sometimes these are very creative and effective. In other cases these very survival strategies may lead to social unrest, sometimes resulting in violence. Given their central role in domestic and neighbourhood life, women especially face the burden of these difficult living conditions, and are vulnerable to particular forms of crime and violent attack.

Women too are resilient and are an important resource towards achieving social cohesion at both the neighbourhood and metropolitan levels. Men and women experience differently, their environments, the issues of safety, protection and the problems encountered in their daily lives as residents, workers, parents and in their social activities. Women can bring their experience to bear on participatory and negotiating processes, often in positive, constructive and creative ways.

## Issue Paper: Integrating the concept of social diversity into public policy
## by Professor Patsy Healey

A major characteristic of our present period is the recognition of the diversity of lifestyles and conditions in our societies. We recognise variations in age, physical capacity, gender, colour, race, culture, interests, place and experience. This recognition is central to what is often called our "post-modern condition". Where once our societies were portrayed as having large numbers of people with similar basic needs, now we see differences in the way these basic needs are manifest and in what people want beyond that. This recognition has been greatly advanced by the growth of women's politics and feminist intellectual endeavour. This has pushed open a window not just on our social lives, but on our working arrangements and the organisation of public policy. Through this window, we have come to see that our societies massively discriminated against women. We have also come to see more clearly the many other discriminations which our ways of thinking and organising brought about because they emphasised homogeneity and universality, not heterogeneity and difference. The policy challenge is now to bring this perception to fruition in our thinking about the city and in all areas of public policy.

This Conference focuses on Women in the City. One of the great successes of our era in Western society is that the voice of women is now much more effectively articulated than in earlier times. One of the deeply ingrained characteristics of Western culture, from Greek civilisation, through the Renaissance, the Enlightenment and the industrial revolution, was suppression of the voice of women. No wonder, having won the vote, women have pushed onwards this century for recognition of much more. Of course, in OECD countries, there has been variable success in this struggle. In some countries, there is still much to be done; in others, women not only have a political voice, they have effective presence in many areas. This presence has helped to generate support systems which make it easier to manage the balance of work, caring, family and leisure activities which are the daily experience of many women. Such support systems have proved beneficial to everyone juggling many roles. But they are still often inadequate, and the burden of managing the complexity of contemporary daily life in cities falls disproportionately on women. The discourse of women's liberation, in all its current richness, helps women understand their natures and the challenges that face them. With these advances in opportunities and understandings, it is perhaps no surprise that in recent surveys, it turns out that women are happier with their lot than men.

An argument is now developing that more attention needs to be given to men's lives, self-conceptions and opportunities, particularly in countries where economic change has devastated the work opportunities in heavy industries where men used to find dignity, political organisation and social status. Unskilled young men have a particularly hard time in some countries just now in finding a role, or any respect from the wider society. Not surprisingly, their response to alienation is often aggressive and violent.[1] This is suggests that the issue of women's roles in public affairs is more than a question of redressing an imbalance. Western societies traditionally unfairly disadvantaged women. Now we must be careful that our societies do not unfairly disadvantage certain groups of men.

Many now redefine the issues of women's participation and needs in the more inclusive form of sensitivity to gender differences. From there, the recognition that women may in some respects (but not always or necessarily) have different perceptions, interests and needs from men widens out into an awareness that people are much more diverse than we seemed to think. But we can understand the issue of opening up our societies to the voice of women in a broader way. While we all knew how varied and variable the people we know are, somehow public policy dealt in the categories of standardised units. We found ourselves treated as aggregates; numbers of households, numbers in work, numbers with children. And that standard unit seemed always to be an average male. This image is encapsulated in urban planning in Le Corbusier's standardised "modular man", whose dimensions were to be at the core of all design, from furniture to city. The challenge today is to displace such homogenising concepts in public policy with a rich recognition of the social diversity of people's situations, lifestyles, wants and needs.

## Women as carriers of the future

Women have a particular responsibility in this context. We must not forget that the modernist project has brought great benefits, in terms of wealth, welfare and opportunity. Without it, current advances in women's wealth and welfare might have been impossible. Yet it was oppressive too. Competitive, atomistic economic rationality has come to dominate our lives and our public policy conceptions. Now that, to use Dear's words,[2] the modernist project has "floated away", we see not only social diversity as being among people; we also realise that there are diverse discourses and forms of social relations, diverse ways of thinking and acting.

Having increasingly found a public voice, women are now important carriers for this appreciation of difference, as well as campaigners on those issues which are particularly associated with the condition of being a woman, for example, childcare, care of the elderly, children's play, reliance on public transport, physical safety and collaborative approaches to governance. While maintaining the unit, the "family", women are paying attention to the interests of diverse members, leading and shaping structures within which members flourish, rather than directing and driving groups of people forward from "on top" or "in front". To the extent that these ways of thinking and doing things are seen as important, both within the economic sphere and in the wider society, women in public affairs are often "carriers of the future". Thus women have come to have a key role in the present period, not just in the process of human reproduction, but in social reproduction, of our economic, political and cultural relations of existence and "human flourishing".[3] This recognition needs to be acknowledged by ensuring that women have a much stronger role in the public sphere of the city, in urban governance.

## Urban and regional planning

This shift can be seen in the development of ideas in my own field, which is centrally concerned with the city, its future and its governance. Many planning policies and regulatory criteria still have locked within them the assumptions of the "modern" age. While technological and organisational innovation constantly changes the material conditions of our lives, the pace of change is slow in our ways of thinking and acting; in the cultures within which these innovations are put to use and made sense of. So those of us who see the need for change, in the opportunities for women as such, and in the ideas which women tend to carry, are always impatient. And our field of urban and regional policy and planning is not particularly in the forefront of thinking on these questions at the present time.[4] This was not always so. As Le Corbusier was constructing his "modular man", radical urban and regional planners were constructing images of alternative social practices within which women could be liberated from the drudgery of household duties, with ideas for the collective management of family support services, as beautifully described by Dolores Hayden.[5]

By the middle of the century, however, the urban and regional planning field had become dominated by the discourse of functionalist modernity. The vigorous efforts in planning in the period after the Second World War, often linked to the introduction of the universalist welfare state, were founded on the image of the nuclear family living in suburban family housing.

Men went to work in the city centre or industrial estate, children went to school in the neighbourhood, and women serviced them both, staying at home, using neighbourhood and district shopping centres and services. Women's lot was aided by improved domestic technology, particularly washing machines and vacuum cleaners. This released more time for better childcare and part-time work. Even in the 1960s, as women began to go to work, it was assumed that they needed primarily part-time and local work opportunities.

"Employment sites are distributed fairly widely and many are located around the perimeter of the city which will reduce the journey to work... The opportunity of local employment will enable residents, particularly mothers, to find work within walking distance of their homes".

Milton Keynes Development Plan 1970 p. 26/41.[6]

Meanwhile, the process of urban policy and planning was dominated by elites and particularly the planner as expert, architect, engineer or economist. It was assumed that the expert "knew best" for our societies. In a respected text on urban renewal in the 1960s, a highly regarded British planner observed the two parent, two child family in Coventry City centre going shopping on a Saturday, and a mother, daughter and granddaughter in the East End of London. He remarked: "we have to decide which kind of family we are to encourage and plan for them".[7]

In the modernist 1950s and 1960s, planning was not only paternalistically for people; it sought to shape people's behaviour in particular ways. By the 1970s, many critical analysts identified the function of this physical and social engineering effort as shaping social relations to "fit" the needs of economic enterprises.

We now look back on this period and congratulate ourselves that we have left it behind. We know that most women of working age in Europe are working. Many households are now headed by women. Work patterns are much more complex than those imagined by the traditional planners and so work journeys are less predictable. Women often travel long journeys for their full and part-time jobs. Meanwhile in the arena of governance, politicians, administrators and experts are no longer accepted as governing on our behalf. Instead, they are under pressure to be "at the service" of the public, working "with" citizens to help them sort out and realise their choices, rather than directing and shaping these choices. In OECD countries, we now talk of the "enabling" local authority.[8] In Forester's image, the expert is presented as "a critical friend" to those seeking advice.[9] Or has it changed so much?

There are by now many reviews of the agenda of issues which need attention in response to women's concerns in urban and regional planning.[10] There are also plenty of examples of innovatory practice. Yet these innovations are uneven and halting. It takes time both to gain acceptance of new ideas and slough off the old. What follows are comments on the areas which we need to keep under critical review if we are to keep up the innovatory pressure.

*Recognising the diversity of physical capacity*

Many women from personal experience are aware of how often the built environment seems like an assault course of difficult physical tasks and danger zones. Women have often been the channel through which the voices of children, the disabled and the elderly have expressed their frustration at these difficulties, because women are so often cast in the role of carer. With more recognition of diversity, there are now in many countries an array of pressure groups campaigning for making the built environment more user-friendly, safe and secure. Building and planning regulation in many countries now commonly include requirements for disabled access, and there is increasing research on what leads to environments which seem to those who feel physically vulnerable (men as well as women) to be reasonably safe to move around in. Similar shifts are occurring in the fields of transport and housebuilding. Such campaigns have achieved the status of normality in policy discourse in many policy areas in many countries. The following extract from a recent British Development Plan gives an example:

> "The requirements of users of a development should be taken into account in its layout and design; and attention should be given to:
> 1. aspects of personal safety and the security of property, particularly at night;
> 2. the access needs of users, particularly people with disabilities, elderly people and people with children; and
> 3. the provision of toilets, baby changing and feeding facilities and public seating where appropriate."
> Sedgefield District Local Plan (Draft, June 1992)
> Policy D2: Design for People

But in practice it is more complicated. One concern relates to the power of the policies and the discourses to influence negotiations with builders, developers and managers. Another concern is the potential conflicts between different pressures. We adjust to the needs of those with prams and in wheelchairs, only to find this creates problems for the blind. Before long, it all becomes yet another area of pressure group politics. This widens the question into the arena of planning processes. How do we discuss the built environment challenges faced by the diversity of human physical capacity? Do we let experts define how to respond to the diversity? Or do we bring in the representatives of the diversity. If the latter, how do we do this and how do we resolve the multiple conflicts and reach creative solutions?

*Demography, household change and work relations*

The number of people living in two-adult households with children in which the male partner is the sole or main breadwinner has seen a dramatic decline in recent years. In Britain, in 1961, 52 per cent of households were married couples with dependent children. By 1991, this had fallen to 25 per cent, including cohabiting couples. Lone person households had risen in the same period from 4 per cent to 26 per cent (General Household Survey 1991). By 1987, 56 per cent of mothers with children of 10 years or more, were working, more than a third of them full time (General Household Survey 1987).

Women are living longer than men, so there are more households of single elderly people. The problems faced by elderly people getting around local environments is very much a problem of women. Social change has also produced more single person households as women strive for autonomy and control over their personal lives, while the rise in single parents and particularly single mothers has resulted both from these pressures and the scale of divorce and family breakdown. In Denmark and Britain, by 1989, 14 per cent of all families with children were lone parent families. In Germany and France the figure was 12-13 per cent, and in Belgium, Luxembourg and the Netherlands it was 10-12 per cent. As a result of these and other pressures, households are more various in their housing demands and needs. Housing and planning policies have had to adjust to these changes in relation to the type and price of housing provided and its location. Meanwhile changes in the economy have drawn more women into the workforce, both in the expanding management and professional sector and in often part-time and low-paid jobs. Increasingly across Europe, levels of economic activity are becoming more similar between the genders and hours worked are converging.

What these trends have done is often to increase the range of responsibilities women have to undertake – parenting, caring for older or disabled relatives, household provisioning and working. One consequence is that women's travel patterns are often complex as they accomplish daily life and generate demand for new and flexible support services (the expansion of childcare, the rise of new services, cleaning, home-delivery of meals, etc. and the expansion of new forms of retail provision, the once a week family shopping trips, or work-based shops and services). Such issues are often included in general Equal Opportunities policies. Urban planning policies can facilitate or impede the complex lives of women (and men) in this position. Other urban management policies can make a difference too. For example, the Commune of Milano is developing a "Policy for time" aimed at making shops, health and social welfare offices open at times more convenient for many women. Within the arena of spatial planning, plans may contain general policies about access and equal opportunities, but it is not necessarily clear what these should involve specifically. For urban and regional planners, these changes mean not only recasting our traditional conceptions of spatial arrangement and transport movements. We need to conduct or sponsor research into how, generally, people are relating their daily life routines and movement patterns as they move around the urban environment and what this implies for policies about where development should go; what services (both physical and social) should be linked to development and about the development of intra-urban transport systems. And once again we have to address the question of how we get to know what spatial arrangements help and hinder people, and how to deal with situations where what helps one, hurts others.

*Environmental care*

The importance of moderating the adverse impact of contemporary economic processes and ways of life on physical and biological natural systems is now widely understood. The European Union (EU), national and local governments all have policies aimed at reducing environmental damage and encouraging resource conservation. Of course we are all, as citizens, implicated in this effort. But women's influence can be important as we discuss how we address the issues involved. The environmental field is one well-populated with experts, natural scientists, engineers and economists. As Hajer argues, there are often major clashes between these experts as to the nature of the "environmental problem" and how to address it.[11] Solutions are typically put forward in terms of calculation (of costs and benefits) and technology. But these debates remain within the discourse of modernism. In particular, they "crowd out" moral and aesthetic views of environmental care. How we value environmental quality is not just a matter of identifying and weighing preferences. It is a result of moral debate on conceptions of the future, of risk, of the relation of people to each other, their descendants, to other species and to natural systems generally. And this is where women come in.

Philosophically, there is a long-standing tradition linking the natural environment and women, "nature and nurture". Planners in Britain earlier this century saw this clearly, as the following quotation illustrates:

"The Town and Country Planning Act (1932) rightly includes the statutory powers to deal with both (town and country). But there should be no attempt at fusion between the two: town should be town and country be country; urban and rural can never be interchangeable adjectives.

...Towards the town all is centripetal, converging on a concentrated and limited area; this concentration must of course be controlled ... but the attitude towards it is identical – from all sides people and interests are converging inwards and ultimately upwards. Towards the country all is centrifugal: with our backs on the town and village we look out in all directions on an ever-widening, opening horizon.

...the English countryside (is) a Ceres, a well-cultivated matron, who duly produces, or should, her annual progeny. If therefore it is true that the town should not invade the country as a town, the regularising hand of man has nevertheless sophisticated the country to serve his needs ... (a) prolonged and profound process of remodelling by human hands" (Patrick Abercrombie, writing in 1933).[12]

We may reject this simple-minded association. Yet the experience of nurturing and of household management is one in which moral principle, emotional sensitivity and material interest are constantly in play together. It is this experience many women can and do bring forward in their approach to the environmental questions, to help us think about balancing what we do now for ourselves with our concern for the future, for others and for other species. This in turn affects what we consider to be costs, benefits and the timescale of their realisation, and our attitude to risks. Consequently, there is a contribution to be made to urban governance by women from our experience on the shaping of environmental policy criteria in our plans and regulations.

*Policy processes: confrontational disputation or collaborative argumentation*

What the above examples emphasise is that bringing women into urban governance and regional planning is not just about shifting the substantive agenda, although this itself is very important. Responding to social diversity is not merely about developing a more sensitive and disaggregated understanding of people's capacity and behaviour, and adjusting our planning policies to accommodate the diversity as far as possible. It also opens up questions about values, about what we prioritise and how. Beyond this, it raises questions about how we discuss our common concerns and our differences, about policy processes.

At one level, many authorities are paying attention to more sensitive consultation strategies, perhaps with more informal discussion arenas, or women-only meetings, where particular cultural traditions make participation in mixed debate difficult (for example, Leicester City Council's approaches in the United Kingdom).[13]

Because of the multiplicity of interests in what happens in places, urban and regional planning systems have long paid attention to questions of process – of how issues are identified, checked out with interested parties, debated, agreed upon and followed through into action. Most systems have provision for some form of public discussion or consultation about plans, policies and/or projects. Whatever the formal arrangements, the policy processes of planning systems have commonly been dominated by the discourses of professionals (architects, engineers, economists, geographers), or of political ideology, or of administrators and lawyers. None of these has been particularly effective in addressing the diversity of interests and values which surround many environmental issues. The processes and discourses chosen may themselves serve to polarise debate and exacerbate confrontation. They also tend to exclude many people from the debating arena, and the understandings and ideas they bring with them. This exclusion may then have political consequences, as those left out continue to challenge decisions, through lobbying activity, the ballot box, and direct protest. In this context, it is not surprising that more attention is now being given to conflict mediation processes in urban and regional planning.[14] However, there are different approaches to such mediation. At one pole, the emphasis is on striking bargains, in the language of calculating the balance of gains and losses to the interests involved. At the other are approaches which seek to encourage mutual understanding, collaborative learning, the collective redefinition of participants' interests, the redefinition of problems, and, in this context, a joint process of invention of appropriate policies and actions. Such collaborative discourse requires skills in mutual tolerance, in listening and learning, in attending to other people's concerns. It is these skills, so Gilligan[15] argues, which have been ingrained in the upbringing of women in western culture. Men, in contrast, have often experienced an upbringing which has encouraged self-centred competition, individual "play to win" strategies and confrontational encounter. It is in this context that bringing women's voices into urban governance processes may help in the search for ways of democratic and collaborative problem solving. And it is not accidental that many of the academics working on such policy processes are women.[16]

## Conclusion

Bringing women into urban governance, then, is partly about a substantive agenda, fostering the escape from "modernity" and the "modular men" and universal standards which have cluttered our field. Outside the modernist "prison", it becomes easy to recognise the different capacities, perceptions and values which people hold. As a marginalised majority, women have both lived experience of marginalisation and the strength in numbers to change this. There are now many strategies for pushing forward women's experience, which range from requiring women to be represented in any policy arena, to setting up women's monitoring groups in organisations aimed at raising policy issues and see that they are followed through. The existence of Committees on Womens' Issues adopted in some local authorities in Britain has been a valuable way of identifying neglected issues and ensuring they have a place on policy and implementation agendas. In some cases planning and other projects are routinely reviewed by such groups in order to identify impacts (for example, in Sheffield City Council and Harlow in the United Kingdom). In this endeavour, women are pushing forward a broader agenda about the recognition of social diversity. Women, because of numbers, can carry forward the voice of other minority groups who have shared in the experience of marginalised, neglected and "crowded out" values and interests.

More than this, however, the experience of many women provides a store of capacities and skills which are particularly valuable at the present time as we search for ways of managing our collective co-existence in shared spaces in the context of our recognition of social diversity. This endeavour lies at the heart of urban governance and at making the conditions of cities more liveable. If we acknowledge the social diversity, we are then faced with major challenges in negotiating collective strategies for managing urban and regional space which not only are accepted as legitimate, but which provide frameworks within which households, firms, associations and agencies can flourish, and contribute to the objectives of economic development, social cohesion and environmental sustainability. This requires collaborative problem-solving, not competitive confrontation. Women, from their experience and that of their mothers and grandmothers, carry many of the skills and capacities which this challenge entails. So, bringing women into urban governance is not just about redressing a balance, letting women "join" the men. It is about creating a different future for all of us, within which the diversity of our lives in cities today is recognised and in which neglected and marginalised capacities and perceptions are allowed to flourish and infuse our thinking about what our cities could be like and how we might collaboratively get there. This implies that women should not linger too long on the particular problems of the position of women; merely long enough to ensure that women are well-represented in all relevant organisational arenas. The next step is to focus on recasting agendas to recognise social diversity and develop styles of democratic collaborative problem-solving. This is the big gain to which our slow steps are currently aiming.

# Notes

1. Campbell, B. 1993, *Goliath*, Methuen.
2. Dear, M. in P. Healey *et al.*, (eds), *Managing Cities* (1995).
3. I am indebted to Chang-Woo Lee, a graduate student in the Department of Town and Country Planning, University of Newcastle upon Tyne, for introducing me to this Korean concept.
4. There is, however, a growing body of research and practice on gender, spatial relations and the physical and natural environment.
5. Hayden, D. 1981, The Grand Domestic Revolution, MIT Press.
6. As quoted in Davoudi, S. 1988, "Planning for Women", MPhil dissertation, University of Newcastle upon Tyne.
7. Burns, W. 1963, New Towns for Old.
8. Batley, R. and Stoker, G. 1991, Local Government in Europe.
9. Forester, J. 1993, Critical Theory, Public Policy and Planning Practice, State University of New York, Albany.
10. For example in Britain see the work of the Women and Geography Group of the IBG, the RTPI's 1988 report on Planning for Choice and Opportunity, and work by Gilroy, 1993, Women and Housing, Avebury; Greed, C. 1994, Women and Planning, Little J. 1994, Gender and Planning.
11. Hajer, M. 1993, The Politics of Environmental Discourse, PhD Thesis, University of Oxford, to be published by Temple Press.
12. From Abercrombie, P. 1933/1944, Town and Country Planning, Oxford University Press, pp. 177/79).
13. As quoted in Calder *et al.*, 1993, Women and Development Plans, Working Paper No. 27, Department of Town and Country Planning, University of Newcastle upon Tyne.
14. For example, Susskind, L. and Cruikshank J. 1987, *Breaking the Impasse: Consensual Approaches to Resolving Public Disputes*, Basic Books, New York Forester, (see note 8 above).
15. See Gilligan, C. 1982, In a Different Voice, Harvard University Press, Cambridge, Manchester.
16. See for example, Judith Innes, Karen Christenson, Jean Hillier, Sue Barrett, and my own work in the English planning literature.

*Chapter 3*

# URBAN POLICIES AND THE PLANNING PROCESS

"Our Motto should be 'linkages'. We should draw links between experts and the grassroots level, to create linkages between the various types of experiments in different regions and countries. We should draw links between the various levels of political power, local, regional and federal, and we should link organisations and organise all these linkages."

**Mrs Helena Vaz da Silva, Member of the European Parliament, Portugal and Chair of the Theme on Women and Urban Policies OECD Conference on Women in the City, Paris, 4-6 October 1994.**

This chapter is concerned with women's participation and the development of a gender perspective in the political arena, the policy process and in planning practice. A key theme that runs through the various sections of this chapter is that of "linkages". In order that the knowledge and expertise of women and men organised at the community level be tapped, and that their interests and concerns are responded to by policy makers and urban planners, it is vital that vertical linkages are made between the various levels of political power – local, regional, national and federal. Equally important is the fostering of horizontal linkages between different organisations and actors involved in urban development: politicians, activists, professionals, employers, users and beneficiaries.

Another key concept for the concerns of this chapter is that of "citizenship" for both women and men, meaning not just political rights, but the right to be able to actively participate in all spheres of activity in city life.

## Women and urban governance

For women to participate in urban policy and planning processes, and for these processes to be made more gender sensitive, a concerted approach is necessary. This requires, in the first instance, improving women's representation in political structures, because reforming urban planning is a political as well as a technical and institutional process. Second, it is necessary that women organised at the community level and in interest-based groups provide a demand-led approach through lobbying and making claims on elected representatives. This in turn requires that women's active participation in organisations outside of government is improved and facilitated. A gender-sensitive approach to the development of new intersectoral urban partnerships is another prerequisite for engendering urban governance and urban management. This requires women themselves to be organised and to play an advocacy role in order for a women's constituency constantly to hold the partnership project to account.

*The issue of "mainstreaming"*

A key issue debated at the Conference was how best to ensure that women's issues are brought into the mainstream of politics and policy development. The representation of women through special ministries, bureaux, desks or departments runs the risk of sectorising women's issues, leaving other ministries or departments free to conduct their business without reference to the contribution or needs of women. Moreover, it also results in the marginalisation of women's issues, as the "women's sector" is usually under-resourced and cannot easily take on "the mainstream".

While there was no dispute over the importance of mainstreaming a gender perspective and women's concerns, there were anxieties expressed by some participants, that by "mainstreaming", women were giving up their "safe spaces". It was felt that there could be a loss of influence as women's issues are added to many others that have to be taken into consideration, and that often the most competent women are creamed off from women's affairs into mainstream departments.

It was concluded that countries with national women's organisations should not dismantle them, but rather change their functions from funding women-only organisations, or implementing women-only projects, to networking with other organisations and institutions representing women, and catalysing within their own governments and constituencies for a gender-sensitive approach to policy and planning. For this to occur, the organised participation of women at the community level is essential, as is the role of women's advocacy in holding the mainstream to account.

This discussion was closely related to the debate on the use of the terminology "women" and "gender". An argument was made that "gender" is too abstract a concept, and that the term "women" is more easily converted into policy. It was concluded that while women organise, participate, and constitute specific political, policy and planning constituencies, a gender perspective (which recognises the different responsibilities of women and men and the social relations between them) is necessary for equitable approaches to policy and planning.

## Women's role and representation in public office

A strongly held view at the Conference was the need for greater representation of women in politics, and this issue was covered in a number of national reports submitted at the Conference. As the former Mayor of Brisbane, Sally Anne Atkinson put it, "there is no substitute for being there", and "the only way to make change happen is to get women into the mainstream of public office and bureaucracy". There are a number of reasons why it should be possible for women to participate in public office. One is

60

democracy. Another is that for real change to occur, it has to be both institutionalised and legitimised by legislation. Also, women have particular experiences of and relationships to the urban environment and they have proved themselves to be effective change agents at the city or local level on a range of issues.

*Problems of increasing women's participation in public office*

There continue to be a number of obstacles to women's engagement in public life, even in countries which have a good record on women's political representation. In some countries, for example Germany and Norway, women's representation although still quite good, is declining, at the national level at least. In other countries such as Finland, women's representation at the local level is on the increase. In Australia five years ago, nearly half the mayors of the capital cities happened to be women. Now there is only one. In the recent local elections in Brisbane the number of women was cut by two thirds. Even when the proportion of women remains fairly constant, there is a high turnover of elected women. The issue, of course, is not a headcount of women and men, but change in political, policy and planning processes to identify and respond to women's needs and to promote women's participation.

One conclusion to be drawn here is that women cannot be complacent. Hard won gains are often rolled back. Another issue is that society has not yet managed to make it easy for women to continue in politics, even when the opportunity exists. This helps explain why women often appear passive when it comes to political life. For women elected representatives to have a sustainable political career and to fulfil a responsibility by standing for public office, women's multiple roles and responsibilities have to be recognised. Moreover, the practice of government has to accommodate these.

The Swedish experience suggests that considerable progress in increasing the participation of women in policy arenas as well as the labour market, was based on the expansion of childcare facilities and parental insurance. These made it possible for both women and men to combine productive and political life with family responsibilities. Thus the are legislative and material prerequisites for women to take part in public life. This is confirmed by the Finnish experience where a system of individual taxation and social security has given legal and practical backing to women's independence, reinforced by the Equal Status Act of 1987 which compels ministries to promote equality between the sexes at work.

*Ensuring gender sensitive local government*

Women are generally better represented at local than at state or national level, although they generally still remain a minority. Some governments or political parties have quota systems to ensure the representation of women, for example the Labour Parties of both Britain and Australia. This was seen by many Conference participants as a positive step forward, although the question of quotas remains a controversial one and it was pointed out that it is not only the number of women in politics that is important, but the contents of policy.

The example of Sweden shows how women's representation can be increased without a compulsory quota system. Currently around half the representatives in the national parliament are women. Strategies to achieve this include making the ratio of women to men visible by presenting regular statistics, establishing concrete, time-bound targets for increasing the proportion of women, and pursuing specific measures to achieve these goals. The pressure of public demand together with political will, means that in Sweden all political parties are committed to increasing the number of women candidates.

There was discussion on the particular role of women in office at the metropolitan or municipal level, and their political responsibility to a women's constituency. This does not come automatically to female representatives in public office. The key factor is whether there are institutional structures to ensure that the specific interests of women are represented by local councils, and whether councillors have transparent, accountable and open channels of consultation and communication with their constituencies.

The Norwegian experience suggests that for local government to be a more effective site of representative democracy involving women, it needs to be decentralised in terms of local taxation and financing, as well as local decision making power. A cautionary note was sounded that in many countries the political will is not there. Local government in particular is about power and about resources. Existing interest groups are unlikely to give these up. Thus increasing the participation of women will remain a battle which will not be won automatically by decentralisation.

---

### Inset 8.   Women's offices in Community Councils, Austria

In City Councils in Austria, attempts have been made over the past five years to institutionalise women's politics. One of their essential aims is to bring gender issues into mainstream debates, thereby raising the awareness of politicians and the public alike. The Women's Offices work at creating equal opportunities for women and men in professional and every-day life, by supporting initiatives and groups for self help. The offices themselves are creating an information base and provide advice, usually in the fields of law, rights and social matters.

In the city of Graz, there are two Women's Offices. The first was founded in 1986. It supports autonomous women's groups and is politically independent. It does not take part in the decision-making processes of the city council. In Vienna, the Office for the Promotion and Co-ordination of Women's Affairs was installed in 1991 as a municipal department of its own and with its own budget. It is supervised by the Executive City Councillor for Education, Youth, Family, Social Affairs and Women's Issues. The Office is not obliged to participate in decision-making and its staff capacity makes this impossible at present, but it aims to insert a gender perspective into every day community politics. An important emphasis is laid on urban planning and housing for women.

*Source:* National Report, Austria, OECD Conference on Women in the City: Housing, Services and the Urban Environment, Paris, 4-6 October, 1994.

*Women's participation and organisation in communities*

Women and men are often interested in different issues organisationally. It is no coincidence, for example, that women are highly represented in social sector ministries such as health, and that at the local level, women take up portfolios on housing and education. This pattern is often replicated at the level of community participation and organisation. Women and men cluster around different interest areas and, as pointed out in the Australian National Report, research shows that women are more likely to participate in community consultation processes than men. Women tend to be more in touch with community issues as they confront them on a daily basis. Women also establish informal neighbourhood networks through their daily living patterns. These networks can be utilised most effectively in urban planning decision-making processes.

---

Inset 9.   **Women's participation in partnerships for housing, Canada**

Canada offers an excellent example of women's successful involvement in participation at the community level. Over the last ten years, women have assumed a significant role in the development, management and ownership of non-profit and co-operative housing. There are now around 60 projects across Canada. Grassroots women's groups have thus emerged as new participants in the housing system. They have obtained funding, found sites, negotiated with architects and builders, selected residents and managed project operations themselves. Through these partnerships and active participation in the co-operative housing movement, women have taken control over their own lives, have learnt marketable skills and exercise greater control over their housing environment.

*Source:* Round Table Discussion, OECD Conference on Women in the City: Housing, Services and the Urban Environment, 4-6 October, 1994.

---

*The relationship between participation and consultation*

From the perspective of communities and women within them, community activism is also an important avenue towards participation in city level urban planning and policy-making processes. In many OECD countries, rhetorical commitment to community consultation is becoming standard procedure for all levels of government. This commitment is usually best translated into effective practice where there is felt to be a strong community interest, a desire to mobilise community support, or where the community itself or interest-based groups within it are well organised. However, it is often the case that women are invisible in the urban planning process. Planners often fail to recognise their specific needs and thus do not consult women or address the problems which are relevant to them. This in turn encourages lack of involvement from women in the community, while planners remain unaware of the impact of their decisions on women's lives.

## Women's advocacy: holding the "mainstream" to account

Mainstreaming gender issues and developing a gender perspective in policy and planning would not have been possible without the organised force of women. Not all women wish to organise autonomously, but many appreciate the women-focused campaigns taken up by women's research and advocacy groups, such as women's health and safety issues, and many of these groups have participated in successful coalitions in support of political change. As indicated above, women cannot afford to be complacent. Constant vigilance is necessary to protect gains that are made, particularly in relation to social policy, but also with regard to political participation.

This provides the strongest argument for the on-going organisation of women as a separate, interest-based political constituency, for example in the form of issue-based organisations, such as women's health coalitions or parent's associations which often involve a majority of women. Alternatively organisation can comprise broader coalitions and networks. The National Congress of Neighbourhood Women in the United States, for example, has as its aim "to build an effective social movement through a national network of locally-based women's groups and individuals that provides mutual support as well as a political and economic power base for grassroots women". At an international level GROOTS (Grassroots Organisations Operating Together in Sisterhood) was formed out of the 1985 Nairobi Conference which concluded the UN Decade for Women, with the purpose of "networking to build a grassroots women's movement into the 21st century".

Whether at a local, national or international level, experience suggests that the organised political power of women will ensure that political parties take seriously the power of the female vote. In Sweden, for example, new women's networks have been recently formed to campaign for better political responsiveness to women. They joined forces and threatened to register themselves as a women's party if the existing political parties did not take women's issues into account more seriously. This challenge, which received excellent media coverage, had the effect of making established political parties place women's issues higher on the political agenda.

### Gender equity in partnerships

Urban partnerships involve a range of actors and require permanent co-ordination between users, designers and decision-makers. Depending on the nature of the objectives, a variety of partners can be involved. Partnerships should ideally be built on shared interests, reciprocal support and mutual benefit, with each partner contributing according to their respective resources, strengths and areas of expertise.

### Inset 10. "Les femmes et la ville", Marseilles, France

The Association Les Femmes et la Ville (Women and the City) was founded in Marseilles in 1990. Its members are researchers in the social sciences, as well as elected representatives and activists from other women's organisations. Together they aim to foster change by understanding the role of women in the city and gender relations in society. In their fight against exclusion of women, the association makes a distinction between the action of the public authorities on behalf of women in the city, and the initiatives taken by the women of Marseilles themselves, either in formal or informal associations, both to put pressure on the authorities, and to help themselves in neighbourhoods and suburbs, in the absence of public support.

Marseilles boasts a wide range of women's organisations, many of which are affiliated to Les Femmes et la Ville. They include local branches of national and international associations such as the Women's Civic and Social Union, Young Women's Christian Association, University Women and the Family Planning Association.

There are also organisations indigenous to Marseilles. The Centre for Guidance, Documentation and Information for Women was created in 1974 and is subsidised by the municipality. It publishes two periodicals which provide a forum for the women of Marseilles to express their concerns. It also provides legal advice and undertakes training and "action-research". Another example is FLORA (Women's Struggle: Autonomous Regional Organisation) which is active in the cultural sphere, organising workshops on writing, cinema and other forms of self-expression by women. The Mediterranean Women's Forum is a highly active forum for dialogue.

At the neighbourhood level there are numerous women's organisations, mainly focusing on the mother-child relationship. Women with school-going children seek opportunities to meet other women. They come together as mothers' groups but this often extends to becoming involved in community responsibilities. Such groups have become very involved in addressing sensitive but pressing issues such as racism and the drugs problem.

The women of Marseilles, through a network of diverse organisations, are actively involved citizens. Awareness and solidarity are growing among them, and they are becoming better and better organised.

---

*Source:* Knibiehler, Y., "Combating Exclusion in Marseilles", paper presented to the OECD Conference on Women in the City: Housing, Services and the Urban Environment, Paris, 4-6 October, 1994.

Reciprocity is built on valuing the respective resources of the partners, whether these are material resources, managerial co-ordination, local information, professional expertise, entrepreneurship or the enthusiasm and energy of residents.

Clearly there is a need to recognise the interests, contributions and reciprocal potential of women as well as men in urban partnerships. One increasingly common approach to democratising and fostering the concept and process of gender sensitive partnership, is to see women as stakeholders, with specific interests and needs. While this can be useful, a potential danger here is to characterise women as a "vulnerable group".

---

Inset 11. **The development of an indicators process for Women in Human Settlements, UNCHS**

The Women in Human Settlements Development Programme (WHSDP) of the United Nations Centre for Human Settlements (Habitat) is developing and co-ordinating an Indicators Process (IP) which began with the elaboration and implementation of a base line survey, aimed at measuring women's participation in the human settlements process at the community level. The survey has been carried out in informal settlements in Sri Lanka, Tanzania, Uganda, Colombia, Ecuador and Costa Rica. Research is current being carried out in Zambia, Ghana and Bolivia. The second phase will involve pinpointing indicators which can measure women's participation at the local and national levels of human settlements development. The development of indicators of women's participation has three objectives:

1. to identify indicators which are useful for measuring women's participation in shelter strategies and which can influence policy;
2. to empower women at the community level through their participation in the collection and analysis of data;
3. to enhance dialogue between professional and grassroots women.

Indicators include women's socio-economic indicators, women's access to services and infrastructure, women's access to land and housing, discrimination against women, and women's participation in decision-making.

Already the task has provided a useful tool for highlighting the potentially powerful role that women play in human settlements development, and the process has succeeded in empowering women to articulate their human settlement needs, as well as those of their dependants. For example, the indicator measuring the extent to which communities are reliant on women's earnings show that in Tanzania, women contribute more than half the total household expenditure while only 22 per cent consider themselves to be the economic head of household. This has given women an idea of how much their economic contribution means to the everyday functioning of their households. Moreover, by disaggregating the data collected by gender, the WHSDP IP believes that the community as a whole benefits from the knowledge, while at the same time promoting equality.

*Source:* Hinchey Trujillo C., "The Women in Human Settlements Development Programme", paper presented at the OECD Conference on Women in the City: Housing, Services and the Urban Environment, Paris, 4-6 October, 1994.

Moreover women en masse cannot be seen as stakeholders as they are far too numerous and diverse to constitute a homogeneous group. Another problem is that gender issues and the presence of both women and men among all stakeholder groups get ignored if women are singled out as one particular group. Finally, the stakeholder approach might identify actors, but does not necessarily address the processes and practices by which urban partnerships are conducted.

*The importance of linkages*

In recognition of the need both to move women's issues into urban institutions and partnerships, as well as to keep local activism robust, strong linkages are needed between

---

### Inset 12. Grassroots women reclaiming and rebuilding community: Neighbourhood Women's Renaissance, United States

Neighbourhood Women's Renaissance (NWR) is a three building, thirty-three unit apartment complex which opened in Williamsburg, Brooklyn on the former Greenpoint Hospital site in 1993. A local group of grassroots women from this multi-ethnic low income community, working in a coalition of neighbourhood organisations, led a ten year campaign to re-develop this site for an innovative community plan to adapt the former hospital to a multi-complex low income housing site which included a nursing home and community medical clinic.

Twelve years later, forty-five units of affordable housing have been built, the majority owned by Neighbourhood Women's Renaissance Limited Partnership (a subsidiary of Neighbourhood Women of Williamsburg/Greenpoint), the only grassroots women's organisation in the city of New York which owns and operates affordable housing. A mixed victory, the housing currently coexists alongside a city-run 400 bed homeless men's shelter on the same complex. Regrettably, most of the innovative women-centred design concepts NWR sought to implement to demonstrate what poor women need to succeed in work and family, were dropped by funding agencies.

The case is an example of the support structures and barriers grassroots women encounter when they initiate a pro-active, comprehensive community development plan to expand local community control over land re-use and abandoned city buildings, and to ensure that women are empowered to own, design and control significant housing resources which reflect the needs of women and their families. As such it provides insights for planners and urban policy makers on the participatory planning, design and financing mechanisms that are needed for low income women to serve as empowered community redevelopers.

*Source:* Schilen, S., "Case Study: Grassroots Women Reclaiming and Rebuilding Community: Neighbourhood Women's Renaissance", paper presented at the OECD Conference on Women in the City: Housing, Services and the Urban Environment, Paris, 4-6 October, 1994.

grassroots organisations and movements, professionals and their organisations, and the decision-makers responsible for policy. The more women are involved at all these levels, the easier it will be to make strong and empowering links. This requires political will based on political pressure from women, and training for professionals so they can develop and employ a gender perspective and an understanding of how far private entrepreneurship can facilitate or hinder the interests of women. In general, better information networks and gender disaggregated data is needed for urban partnerships and city planning which is gender sensitive.

Urban partnerships are potentially the vehicle through which bottom-up efforts can intersect or dovetail with top-down approaches. It is vital not only that women participate, but that the partnership process is responsive to the interests and needs of women. This includes accommodating the needs of women who have to balance multiple responsibilities and who cannot always fit into established meeting formats and times. It also means recognising that women are not always able to participate with the same skill in male-dominated forums. Thus to be gender sensitive, the ways in which urban partnerships are pursued have to be alert to the different approaches that women and men adopt in organisation, negotiation and planning as a result of their socialisation and experience of public life.

The way in which women have to balance multiple activities and responsibilities in their everyday life is different from the way in which men organise their time. So instead of a linear or compartmentalised approach, women tend to be more pluralistic. This approach can be more appropriate for the problems facing urban partnerships which are often multi-faceted and inter-sectoral. Accommodating women in urban partnerships therefore, is a value added rather than an altruistic exercise.


**Planning with a gender perspective**


Women often experience and use the urban environment in different ways from men. Women are more likely to be on low incomes than men and they are disproportionately affected by unsatisfactory housing and poor urban design. Women depend more on public transport and walking than on private cars. Women are most likely to be the ones looking after young children, elderly or sick relatives and women do most of the convenience shopping. Working women usually combine paid work with these domestic responsibilities. Women do not always experience cities as safe places, and are forced to change their lifestyles for fear of crime and violence. For these reasons, women want access to different kinds of services and facilities than men. In particular, women want a safe environment and better transport systems (Takmaz Nisancioglu, 1994).

Despite this, women's needs as users of cities rarely feature in urban planners' policies or projects. This is hardly surprising when women on the whole, are excluded from urban planning decision making processes. There is a strong argument, therefore, for women to be consulted and for participation by women in the planning process, so that the gendered needs of both women and men are addressed.

*Enhancing women's community participation in planning*

Ms. Sule Takmaz Nisancioglu who was Women's Issues Officer in Haringey Council's Town Planning Service (United Kingdom) offered the Conference the following guidelines to increase the participation of women in decision-making:

- it is important first to collect and disseminate information about women to show that women and men have different needs;
- recognise diversity and that women are different, not only from men but from each other.

From the point of view of action, consult with women in order to make them visible. This cannot be done through the traditional public participation exercises as a number of things need to be considered, such as timing of meetings, accessibility of the meeting place by public transport, availability of creches and the translation of materials to ethnic minority languages.

Also, the planning process has to be demystified. It can seem a bureaucratic and complicated process with a life of its own involving technical staff, lawyers, architects and developers, all of whom can act as barriers against the involvement of women from the community. Organising workshops for community groups to explain how planning works and using accessible tools, can enhance the active participation of women in the process.

Special projects for women can be an important way of increasing the awareness of planners on women's issues. Planners and the community can be brought together to develop links around a specific issue which is of particular concern to a section of the community, such as young mothers with children in overcrowded housing. Developing links around such issues makes planning more relevant to women and increases their understanding of how the system works. However, one-off projects, on their own, are

---

**Inset 13.  A cookbook for grassroots planning:
an accessible planning tool, Norway**

The Ministry of Environment in Norway has addressed the issue of demystifying the planning process by publishing a "cookbook" to introduce the new Planning and Building Act of 1985, and to make local land use planning more accessible to women and more commonplace. In the Foreword to the booklet, the Minister writes:

Planning can be complicated, and is often made more complicated than necessary for the express purpose of hindering broad participation. Those in power are not always interested in letting others take over their authority. But if we are to improve society, women must be allowed more control over the shaping of our society.

*Source:* Ministry of Environment, "A Cookbook for Grass-roots Planning", Norway, 1994.

insufficient to shake deep-seated views on gender. Thus it is important to keep the communication channels open, to allow women to put their views across over time. The whole process was represented as follows:

Figure 1. **Participation of women in urban planning decision-making process**

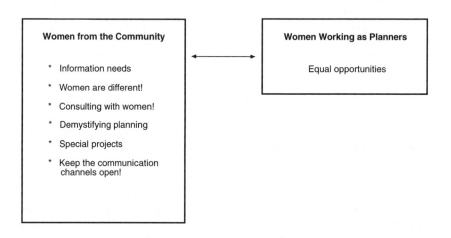

*Source:* Takmaz Nisancioglu S., "Participation of Women from the Community in the Urban Planning Process", paper presented to the OECD Conference on Women in the City: Housing, Services and the Urban Environment, Paris, 4-6 October, 1994.

## Women planners: opportunities and constraints

Women professionals are crucial to the process of achieving gendered cities and of getting women's voices heard. Yet they are still in a minority and in many contexts occupy low grade jobs, with little chance of affecting planning decisions. Nevertheless, the role played by women working as architects and planners is vital to making cities work for women as well as men. Without their view, planning itself suffers.

That this is now recognised as an important area is evidenced by a number of recent conferences. In July 1993 in Melbourne, Australia, a National Conference on "Women and Planning" was held. In Ornskoldsvik, Sweden in March 1994, a Conference was organised by the Council of Europe, entitled "Role and Representation of Women in

Urban and Regional Planning: Aiming at Sustainable Development''. The conclusions from this seminar were presented at the Tenth European Conference of Ministers for Regional Planning in Oslo in September 1994, and were adopted, with a commitment to include the need for women's participation in their activity programme for the next three years.

The representative of the Women and Human Settlements Development Programme of the United Nations Centre for Human Settlements (Habitat) pointed out the importance of enhancing women's participation in urban planning and development, and in particular, of integrating gender into the preparatory phase and the actual activities for the Habitat II Conference which will be held in Istanbul in 1996.

---

### Inset 14. **European Charter for Women in the City**

The Equal Opportunities Unit of the Commission of the European Communities has sponsored a proposition for a European Charter for Women in the City which aims at conceiving a new philosophy in town planning, likely to make a constructive contribution to a true democratic debate which will take account of the needs and the various expectations of citizens, women and men alike. Efforts for revitalising cities must merge with other, newer, political and economic priorities aiming at increased social harmonisation. The issue at stake is to recreate spaces and close social ties with increased equal opportunities for women and men in urban and rural life.

The Charter is composed of the following twelve points:

1. *Women in the City and **Active Citizenship***
   Active citizenship must be approached on the one hand through careful consideration of the influence of dwelling place and on the other, of how representative authorities and economic and political mechanisms in the city work.
2. *Women in the City and **Decision Making and Parity in Democracy***
   Women must at all times be associated in decision-making processes regarding town planning, urban space, housing, transport and environment.
3. *Women in the City and **Equal Opportunities***
   Equal opportunities must be promoted in education and research, in the work places and in all professions related to town and country planning, urban space, housing, mobility and safety in cities.
4. *Women in the City and **Participation***
   Egalitarian participatory processes must be set up for women which will favour renewed ties of solidarity.
5. *Women in the City and **Daily Life***
   Daily life as seen through a woman's eyes must become a political issue,

*(continued on next page)*

*(continued)*

6. *Women in the City and* **Sustainable Development**
   Women must be fully involved in policies for maintaining the ecological equilibrium on our planet.
7. *Women in the City and* **Social Safety and Mobility**
   Every woman, and particularly underprivileged or isolated women, must have access to public transport in order to circulate freely and to fully enjoy economic, social and cultural life in the city. Women too have a right to the city.
8. *Women in the City and the* **Right to Housing and Dwelling**
   Women are entitled to adequate housing.
9. *Women in the City and* **Gender Issues**
   Gender issues in the city must be acknowledged as the source for a newly shared culture and should influence a new town and country planning philosophy.
10. *Women in the City and* **Education and Local Experimentation**
    Gender issues in cities must be taught in schools, institutes for architecture and town planning, and in universities. Experimentation in cities is urgently needed if any changes are to occur.
11. *Women in the City and the* **Role of the Media and Transmitting Experience**
    The media must set out to spread messages which will counteract stereotypes and show women in roles reflecting their development and emancipation.
12. *Women in the City and* **Networks**
    Exchanging information through a European network will promote the Charter and implement action of its principles.

*Source:* Minaca M., Paper presented to the OECD Conference on women in the City: Housing, Services, the Urban Environment, Paris 4-6 October 1994.

*Constraints facing women in planning*

In 1993, the Swiss Regional Planning Office launched a research project about the limited participation by women in municipal planning processes. There are few cases in which more than 20 per cent of municipal council members are women. The project focused on the municipalities as they have considerable power in Switzerland and are of great importance as a gateway to politics.

Many reasons emerged for the limited participation of women. One was that it is difficult for lay people to understand the intricacies of the planning process, and for citizens, both women and men, to see how they are affected by planning decisions. Moreover, it is not only from the women's side that there are obstacles. Men act as effective gatekeepers to the planning process. There is still prejudice in Switzerland against politically active housewives or young mothers, and women are not considered capable of co-operating in technical matters such as planning, and are not approached in this regard (Michel, 1994). Women planners and architects are trained in institutions, where the curricula are gender-blind. They themselves then emerge from such institutions unaware that women and men use the city in different ways.

*Support for women planners*

If more women are going to enter planning and architecture, and this is clearly desirable, they must be given proper support. Michel (1994) makes a number of suggestions in this regard:

- the planning process should be open to participation so that women will realise that they are involved;
- at least two and preferably more women are needed on planning committees;
- women's groups or associations should be systematically included in municipal hearings and in the planning field;
- discussions must allow women to have their own particular say, and the planning process must not be too directive or bureaucratic.

The more women have the courage to express their interests in planning issues, the easier it will be for the individual woman. It is exhausting and frustrating to work alone and this soon leads to resignations or women giving up.

*The importance of women's organisations*

Women planners have few role models and little professional support. They do not have an easy time on planning committees and within the profession and on their own they can do very little. Professional women's organisations can play an important role in overcoming this constraint. For example, in Sweden there is a network called the Women's Building Forum which is a national, politically independent association which is open to all women interested in planning, building and maintenance questions. It has local networks in several Swedish cities, and works for women's experiences to be taken into account, and for women's interests to be satisfied when areas are planned, built and changed. The association also tries to influence public opinion through measures such as articles, exhibitions, participation in housing fairs and establishing prizes for best practice (Sweden, National Report, 1994).

However, women's planning and professional organisations are not always to be found. In Iceland, for example, there are no special women's associations or women's groups within the societies for architects and planners. There is a majority of women working as architects for city planning in the city of Reykjavik, the mayor of which is a woman, and yet they feel they have little influence on design. Moreover, some women architects consider it impossible to separate the views of men and women architects, particularly when women are not involved in specific women focused activities, or efforts to encourage the participation of women (Iceland, National Report, 1994). In such cases, women's groups at community, local or regional level, can often provide strong support for politically active or professional women when organisational or partnership linkages are made.

## Inset 15.  Women's planning networks in Australia

At the Women and Planning Conference, held in Melbourne in July 1993 the establishment of an Australian women's planning network was discussed, and much hard work has culminated in the establishment of the Women's Planning Network in Victoria.

The aim of the Women's Planning Network, Victoria is to:

• identify issues and appropriately respond to promote a public response and provide a supportive network for women involved, and interested in planning issues.

The Network's objectives include:

• to create a dynamic, creative and supportive network for women in planning and related fields;
• to encourage women to participate in professional, government and other forums, representing the planning needs and perspectives of women;
• to encourage Federal, State and Local Governments, the land and development industry and the community sector to recognise women's specific needs and perspective in relation to planning policy and processes.

The Women's Planning Network has been operating successfully in Queensland since 1992. The Network recently completed a project which, through a series of consultations with Queensland women, sought to explore a women's perspective on planning – the processes, systems and outcomes:

The primary aims of the process were to increase women's awareness of the role of planning and its influence on their lives and environments, and empower individual women to participate more fully in the planning debate. The final report will expose government bodies, professional planners and academics to the views and aspirations of women in relation to their communities and acknowledge the extent to which women already influence these areas (Women's Planning Network, 1994-7).

The project concluded with a conference which produced a series of recommendations to address a range of issues discussed at the conference. The broad themes included transport; access to the planning system; feminising the planning process; the environment; and building communities (Women's Planning Network, 1994:39-40).

*Source:* Communication provided by the Government of Australia.

## Gender competence in urban planning

The burden of fostering gender sensitive urban development and making our cities liveable environments for diverse populations should not fall on women planners alone. On the contrary, the development of gender planning competence on the part of all urban professionals is vital. This would include conducting a gender analysis of the problem, the participants and the partners. It would ensure consultation with a diverse range of people, even if that meant employing special planning tools and taking additional time to reach some categories of women and other "invisible" groups. Planning with a gender or diversity perspective does not come "naturally" to professionals, whether women or men, and planning bodies and local governments need to be encouraged to provide training for career and skills development along these lines.

An important suggestion arising out of the Conference was the need to introduce a gender perspective into university curricula for urban planners and related disciplines. This would ensure that gender and diversity issues were not seen as an "add on", but as an integral part of good planning practice. Related to this is the need to integrate gender issues into regular planning procedures and tools. An example was given of the way in which environmental impact assessments and social impact statements can be used effectively to include a gender perspective, and to slowly develop a gender aware regulatory framework.

Another way of establishing gender awareness in planning interventions is to intro-duce a gender perspective into urban policy research agendas (see Annex 1). This means identifying how the issues and ideas which come out of conferences such as this one, might be translated or incorporated into an urban policy research agenda. It also means identifying the institutional frameworks and entry points through which this can take place. In Australia, for example, the forthcoming Urban and Regional Development Review presents an ideal opportunity for introducing gender issues. The UNCHS (Habitat) contribution on establishing indicators of women's participation in community and human settlements development, also offered an exciting example of how both research and policy are crucial areas of intervention for introducing gender concerns.

A key issue in research is stressing the linkages between economic, social and environmental policy. Recognising the interaction between the organisation of work and other social relationships and responsibilities is necessary to the development of sustaina-ble urban development strategies. Women and men are never just workers but have other social roles in the household and community. Thus planning for social diversity means seeing people not just as workers, but also as clients and consumers. While planners compartmentalise different spheres of activity, people do not. Integrated and multi-sectoral approaches to urban development present opportunities for planners to respond to the complexities of peoples' lives, and to recognise gender differences. However, women organised at different levels still need to hold the process to scrutiny, to ensure that gender competent planning is operationalised.

## Planning for everyday life

Rapid socio-economic and political changes in many countries, and the globalisation of economies have resulted in local uncertainties. Even the philosophy of growth, produc-tivity and efficiency which has dominated planning until recently, is being questioned as a result of the emphasis on social and ecological sustainability. The planning process itself is also experiencing something of a crisis. Given rapid social change, it is increas-ingly difficult for decision-makers and planners to predict, to forecast and to plan, even in the medium-term. Moreover, urban societies are becoming ever more heterogeneous and personal ethics are changing. Policy makers are often no longer in tune with the individuals they govern. Linear thinking, one-way communication and top-down planning are no longer appropriate in multifaceted communities with changing values.

In this context, women represent a valuable reservoir of knowledge, skills, sensitivity and overall capacity. The particular concerns of women and the kinds of approaches they adopt in organisation, problem-solving and planning in their everyday lives. In the domestic sphere and in managing the defects and dysfunctions of our cities women's skills are ignored or undervalued. They could be mobilised for the benefit of all, to contribute to the adaptation of planning and decision-making processes to better reflect the complexities of social identities and interaction, and the realities of everyday life.

Our everyday lives are shaped by forces which are partly regulated by globalisation, by the market, by party politics and by national and sectoral planning. The consequences for everyday life of decisions made in these arenas, are often not foreseen. The Scandinavian experience of Planning for Everyday Life was shared with the Conference by delegates from Norway, Sweden and Finland. Their approach confronts these issues at the local level, and is concerned with directing development planning from a starting point of what everyday life is like at the household and community level. Through this focus, planning becomes concerned with how everyday lives are organised, how tasks are connected, how employment is distributed and how the environment is protected. It is concerned with grassroots participation because the valuable experience which exists at local level is recognised. Because women are pivotal to the organisation and management of everyday lives, in Norway this approach has been deemed planning from women's perspective. In Finland, this approach involved children in the planning process. In Sweden, the Women's Building Forum, adopting this approach, came up with concrete gender-sensitive proposals for "the good city".

*Municipal planning on women's terms*

In Norway, although municipalities have increasing responsibilities, they have diminishing resources, leading to demands for greater efficiency. In this context, municipalities are striving to develop a more holistic and inter-sectoral approach to planning. A project was initiated by the Ministry of Environment and the Norwegian Association of Local Authorities, called "A Woman's Perspective in Public Planning – Municipal Planning on Women's Terms" (Mathisen, Skjerven and Husabo, 1994).

Six selected municipalities were asked to participate in the project and they formed a project group of seven or eight members, comprising women from the municipality, from grassroots organisations, from politics and from the administration. The municipalities had to undertake, by political decision, to implement planning processes in ways which incorporated women's perspectives and which bound them in municipal plans. A unique feature of the project was working from the bottom up, but in close contact with the municipal administration.

Output from the project has included both the "Cookbook for Grass-roots Planning" and "A Manual for Alternative Municipal Planning". The first publication represents an attempt to make planning more accessible and less remote, and to promote organisation and lobbying. The second sums up the experience gained from the project. In addition to spreading knowledge to other municipalities in Norway, dissemination of the project has now extended to other countries in Scandinavia and Europe as well.

The results showed less emphasis on material values and more concern for human values. Women's involvement in the planning process also produced the following results:

- stimulation of local initiative and resources;
- solutions that meet people's everyday needs;
- strengthening of local democracy;
- best use made of community resources;
- achievement of more general support for planning and plans.

With regard to replication, it was pointed out that in Norway women have a comparatively high representation in political bodies and organisations (30-40 per cent) and the system for local planning is based on a decentralised model. Furthermore, most municipalities are small and the larger ones can be subdivided. Finally, planning in Norway is no longer dominated by traditional physical and economic planning, making a holistic approach more feasible (Mathisen, Skjerven and Husabo, 1994).

*Building "The Good City"*

In Sweden the Women's Building Forum presented a programme of concrete proposals and ideas which characterise "the good city", some of which are:
- organisation of the city to facilitate the smooth functioning of everyday life, such as a mix between working places and housing, housing for all phases of the lifecycle, and a good public transport network;
- a housing environment that facilitates socialising and co-operation;
- a physically and psychologically healthy environment including open spaces where one is secure and paths where there is no danger of attack;
- good management of financial and natural resources and the facilitation of recycling and re-use;
- harmonious housing design which need not be more expensive but which can improve comfort and aesthetics;
- neighbourhoods which promote responsibility and involvement of all citizens.

The Swedish perspective is that while women's perspectives are often concerned with qualities concerning everyday life, women do not have a monopoly on promoting such qualities. "The good city needs many promoters, one of which is the Women's Building Forum" (Sweden, National Report, 1994).

*The Scandinavian new everyday life approach in Finland*

In Finland, also under the auspices of the Minister of the Environment, the "Scandinavian New Everyday Life Approach" was adopted in 1992, and applied to various local projects dealing with housing and services. According to the Finnish National Report (1994):

"The New Everyday Life" project is a vision, theory and model of action for reorganising the basic tasks of daily life in a manner that enhances the experience of reality as manageable and meaningful. It is also a critique of the present conditions. It questions the functionalist tradition of urban planning and policies, the gaps in representational democracy, the disregard of different competences of men and women, adults and children, and the inability of centralised solutions to solve everyday problems. The "New Everyday Life" is also a vision of a more harmonious, creative and just society in which the reproduction of human beings, nature and culture is not subjugated to the interests of economics and production. The vision paints a mosaic-like society of various self-governing local units."

As a practical enterprise the aim is to organise the structural basis of everyday life in neighbourhoods in a more integrated way.

The central concept of the "New Everyday Life" project is action at the intermediary level – a structure between the state or public sector, the market or private sector, and households. The intermediary level mediates between the public and private and the formal and informal spheres of life. It enables reproduction, production and male and female cultures to be organised in new ways. In practical development terms, the intermediary level can be a neighbourhood or part of a municipality or town and the aim is for such a unit to become an integrated functional, social, organisational, economic and even political unit.

*Some caveats*

The Scandinavian examples demonstrate that planning does not have to be **for** women, children or the elderly, but that it can be done **by** women, children and the elderly. These examples, together with those of women's networks elsewhere, also show that women are demanding more space for ecological and social issues in the planning context. Women often have a particular interest in the urban environment because they have to confront it and manage it on a day-to-day basis. However, care should be taken not to fall into an essentialist argument that women have a "special relationship" with nature or the environment.

A second issue is that although there was a lot of enthusiasm for the Everyday Life approach to planning, some notes of caution were sounded. One problem identified was that community planning or neighbourhood level initiatives are seen by some male planners as the "soft option", or a substitute for real decision making. Thus there is a danger that promoting local level initiatives may result in women being excluded from other levels of decision-making.

A third issue is that the Everyday Life perspective is looking at the city from the point of view of the household – moving from the kitchen to City Hall – which is similar to the approach of Ebenezer Howard and can be seen to be normative. The difference is that for Howard, it was a male-headed household. The challenge is to use the everyday life perspective to understand not only women as a single category, but a wider diversity of interests, operating both at the level of the household and also at the level of the city itself.

*Chapter 4*

# CREATING LIVEABLE ENVIRONMENTS

"Housing and neighbourhood environments have always been designed with women and children in mind, but the minds have been those of male planners and architects. Now the minds are changing! Women professionals, community activists, workers and residents are increasingly asserting their own urban agenda. Women are and will continue to be leading agents of change in the contemporary city."

**Professor Renate Howe, Deakin University, Australia and Chair of the Theme on Housing and Neighbourhood Environments Designed with Women and Children in Mind, OECD Conference on Women in the City, Paris, 4-6 October 1994**

Liveable environments are those which facilitate creative human activities and which promote well-being. They include housing as well as the residential environment. Both influence people's health, welfare, prosperity and the quality of life. Many neighbourhoods of our cities are blighted by economic contraction and social deprivation. They are characterised by increases in unemployment, crime and poverty, and decaying infrastructure and services. The lived environment impacts differently on women and men. Housing must be designed within community settings and with access to services, employment, public transport, leisure facilities and social and cultural amenities.

The intersection of age and gender can have profound effects on how urban life is experienced. For example, adequate housing for the elderly is a growing problem, and one which particularly affects women who are more likely to find themselves "home alone" in their latter and more frail years. Young boys in deprived neighbourhoods find themselves caught up in abusive and violent worlds in ways which are quite distinct from those of teenage girls. It is important to recognise the different interests and needs of both women and men in the design, use and management of housing and the urban environment, and at various stages of their lives.

The problems of inadequate housing, disintegrating neighbourhoods, social divisions, conflict and environmental degradation are increasingly being tackled by social renewal programmes. They are usually conducted by way of a multi-sectoral approach to urban development, which can often serve to highlight women's needs (particularly in relation to housing and health care) and frequently rely on women's involvement (especially at the community level). However, a more consistent approach to gender integration across all components of social renewal remains a goal.

This is a key issue because women tend to spend more time than men in the home and residential neighbourhoods, particularly at certain stages in their lives. Thus the negative impact on women of dysfunctional environments and bad urban planning is severe. Creating liveable environments that cater for women's needs, therefore, is a legitimate goal in its own right. Women constitute an important reservoir of knowledge, skills and understanding of their lived environments and have much to contribute to the design and delivery of housing and to improved city planning.

*Partnerships for neighbourhood betterment*

Women, however, have to juggle multiple responsibilities and need to overcome handicaps such as lack of confidence or skills, in order to participate in public life. Moreover, all too frequently women are included in urban partnerships only at the implementation stage and remain excluded from the formulation, design and allocation stages of programmes and projects. New forms of partnership, therefore, need to adopt an enabling approach. This should foster, on the part of all parties involved, a commitment to developing inter-organisational relationships conducive to genuinely participatory processes that includes both women and men, and at all stages. There are examples from France, such as the Charter for Partnerships for the Development of Distressed Areas, where the value of participation by women is recognised. Genuine participation by diverse groups means reconceptualising the meaning of "successful organisation" and defining new contractual procedures (Dazelle, Cucchiarini 1994).

## Housing and the neighbourhood environment

The discussion on housing and neighbourhood had three main areas of focus. First was the role of women themselves in the design and planning of housing and neighbourhoods. Second was the issue of access to and affordability of secure housing for women. And third, the discussion focused on the increasing diversity of interests and needs in relation to housing.

*Access to housing and earnings*

Access to affordable housing is predicated upon economic power, represented by employment and earnings, or access to housing finance. It is also framed by household size and composition and by relationship formation and reformation. There are gender dimensions to these factors which weigh heavily on women and which are elaborated on below.

Women's labour force participation and income earning opportunities are invariably combined with primary responsibility for domestic work and care of children and other family members. Moreover, they are often located in segments of the labour market which are insecure and, in comparative terms, poorly paid. These factors act as constraints on accessing adequate housing for many women.

While lack of access to secure and affordable housing may be an **outcome** of economic disadvantage, decent housing also is a key **input** in providing women with the capacity to gain access to labour force participation. This is the case "both in the geographical sense, through the location of their housing and its proximity to appropriate local labour markets; and in the socio-emotional sense", (Cass, 1994) in that it provides the stability and security necessary for initiating and sustaining employment and career development.

*Household composition and family formations*

Globally the variety of household types is not always recognised or responded to by architects and urban planners. In many countries, family composition is increasingly varied and relationship formations and reformations are undergoing considerable change. In particular, the rise in the number of lone parent families and single person households, many of them women, is noteworthy. These phenomena have implications not only for housing finance and the distribution of housing benefits, but also housing and neighbourhood design.

**Women and housing design**

Changes in demography, in the family and in women's participation in the workforce all have major ramifications for the design and management of homes, neighbourhoods and cities, which as currently constituted, often no longer reflect the reality of many people's lives. The division of women's lives into public and private spheres remains the major determinant of housing and neighbourhood design. In turn, it serves to marginalise and isolate women in cities. This division can no longer be sustained. As women's participation in the paid workforce continues to rise, location in relation to employment is as important for women as it is for men.

Moreover, rapid changes in global production processes and the increase in "contracting out" and "home work", mean that paid work, domestic labour and leisure activities are no longer spatially discrete. They often take place under the same roof and that roof is the home. This growing phenomenon needs to be taken into account in housing design and by zoning regulations, which often forbid commercial or productive activities to be undertaken in residential areas. This renders illegal, activities undertaken out of economic necessity. The impacts of technological changes and "information highways" also need to be taken into account.

---

### Inset 18.   The "Frauen-Werk-Stadt" Project, Vienna, Austria

The "Frauen-Werk-Stadt" Project was initiated by the Municipal Department for Promotion and Co-ordination of Women's Affairs in 1992. It was intended to create a suburban area for Vienna exclusively planned and designed by women experts, and using women's everyday life as the essential criterion of design. The vehicle for achieving these aims was to commission women architects to design a women-friendly public housing project, based on the guidelines of the Viennese Housing Promotion Act. The winning entry was the master project submitted by Franziska Ullmann, whose design reflected the following:

- well lit, transparent, covered links between the interior and exterior of the building to avoid danger zones, as well as courtyards and garden squares for protected play;
- provision of often neglected "arrangements" such as rooms to store bicycles and prams, and laundry rooms easily accessible on the ground-floor;
- the creation of "social space" to avoid anonymity and to enhance neighbourly relations;
- a strong focus on safety, including an open-structured underground garage with natural lighting, and well lit staircases, each with its own access;
- in the flats themselves, kitchens were large and designed as central places of housework, and all faced the courtyards or common play areas; all flats were equipped with some individual open space.

---

*Source:* Bauer U. and Kail E., "Design of Housing Estate by Women", OECD Conference, Women in the City: Housing, Services and the Urban Environment, 4-6 October, 1994.

*Accessing affordable housing*

Access to employment, level of income and access to secure and affordable housing are closely interrelated. For example, couples are more likely to participate in home purchase than single householders. For lone parent families, predominantly headed by women, low income militates strongly against home ownership. Instead, they are reliant on public and private rental housing. Housing affordability is also very closely linked to tenure type. Women-headed families are over represented in the rental market, bearing the relatively high costs of private rent.

*Housing finance*

Housing finance has largely failed to keep pace with changing labour market trends, particularly the rise in part-time and casual employment. As women predominate in these jobs, and as they form the greatest proportion of single households and lone parent families, they confront outmoded regulations and practices governing housing finance. For couples and two-parent families, women's earnings, added to those of a partner, are often vital for retaining mortgage repayments, particularly during periods of high interest rates. This is so even if women are secondary income earners in part-time work. Thus women's labour force participation has proved crucial for maintaining a culture of private home ownership in countries such as Australia, Canada, the United States and the United Kingdom.

*Rental housing*

The most affordable housing for low income families is generally public rental housing. However, it invariably reaches only a small minority. For many, the only alternative is the private rental market. In the case of single mothers, the very high private rental costs can absorb an inordinate proportion of their income. Cass (1994) estimates for Australia, that in 1988 58.6 per cent of lone mothers spent 50 per cent or more of their weekly income on rent. In Canada, in every age group, women-headed households are much more likely to be renters than their male counterparts (Canada Mortgage and Housing Corporation, 1994). Thus, women are more likely to suffer when the rental market is weak and poorly developed.

In the United Kingdom, young single mothers are routinely housed in "bed and breakfast" hotels, often for long periods, before more secure accommodation becomes available. The damaging effects of such forms of transitional accommodation are not only material but psychological. Sole parent families are often accommodated in establishments which are totally unsuitable to child-rearing and rather than venture out, young women remain closeted in tiny rooms with young children. In Canada, community groups have drawn attention to the prevalence of discrimination and harassment of women tenants by landlords or janitors.

*Security of occupancy*

Another key issue, particularly for low income families is to ensure housing which is not just affordable but which is accompanied by security of occupancy. This is related to income security and appropriate housing finance mechanisms. It is also related to tenure, tenancy agreements and to other regulatory mechanisms. In Canada, for example, there has been a challenge to exclusionary zoning practices which restrict the types of house-holds that are able to live in particular zoned areas. These practices often favour couples and discriminate against sole parents and people in alternative household arrangements.

Some success has already been achieved and such exclusionary zoning was banned in the Province of Ontario in 1989 (Canada Mortgage and Housing Corporation, 1994). On-going challenges in Canada are being made on human rights grounds. This is entirely consistent with the call being made by Habitat International Coalition and other network-ing organisations in the human settlements field: that housing is a human right. This has recently been echoed by the Women and Human Settlements Development Programme (WHSDP) of UNCHS (Habitat).

---

Inset 19.  **Why should human settlements be a major concern
at the fourth World Conference on Women? UNCHS**

Because the development and maintenance of our "HUMAN HABITAT" is an essential part of the struggle for equality, development and peace! Women ... especially in the developing countries of the world, but increasingly so also in the developed countries, struggle daily to eke out an existence for their families. The lack of "humanly adequate" housing and infrastructure ... make women's roles more burdensome and often dangerous because housing is a **basic human right**, which is, however, not adequately recognised or enforced.

---

*Source:* United Nations Centre for Human Settlements (Habitat), WHSDP Discussion Paper for the UN 4th World Conference on Women, Beijing, 4-15 September 1995.

---

*Policy responses*

A key policy issue coming out of the conference was the need to assist women to become credit-worthy, particularly in relation to housing finance. This involves not only providing women with decent access to credit institutions, but designing housing finance that reflects and responds to the realities of women's working and domestic lives.

### Inset 20.  **Australian model code for residential development**

The aim of AMCORD is to facilitate the supply of better, more appropriate housing, to meet the needs of changing lifestyles,to reduce the cost of housing, and to improve housing design. The achievement of these aims will specifically impact on the needs of women in the following and other areas:

Housing choice: greater choice allows for better matching of lifestyle to housing, which is particularly relevant to women as sole parents or living alone.

Consultation: encouragement of community consultation in policy and decision making gives women an opportunity to ensure that policy decisions reflect their interests and needs and those of the community.

Affordability: encouraging best practice in housing design and construction results in lower housing costs which benefits women who, on average, earn less than men.

Environment Design: AMCORD encourages development that provides reasonable access to community facilities which benefits women without transport and who are primary care givers in their own home.

_Source:_ National Report, Australia, OECD Conference, Women in the City: Housing, Services and the Urban Environment, 4-6 October 1994.

Based on the Australian experience, Cass (1994) identifies some key policy issues to be considered. These are in response to biases in access to secure and affordable housing, based on gender and family relationships:

- addressing the issue of affordability of housing for women-headed households and other low and middle income households, including households whose earnings are disrupted by unemployment, illness, disability and sole parenthood;
- addressing the issue of security of occupancy, which is of particular importance for households with children and for the aged;
- addressing the issue of the appropriateness of housing at different stages of the life-course;
- recognising that a house is not only a dwelling but a location, and that the accessibility of housing to jobs, public transport, community services, education and training is a critical issue for women.

### *Responding to diversity in housing needs*

Responding to diversity in housing needs requires that architects, planners and urban development practitioners, whether they are women or men, adopt both a social diversity and gender perspective in their work.

Gender intersects with other social relations such as those based on age and ethnicity. As far as the age variable is concerned, the gendered nature of ageing is discussed below. At the other end of the life cycle, childhood and adolescence are also fundamentally gendered experiences, and yet this is not always recognised. There are numerous youth clubs, for example, which have been provided for young people by planners, but which have been occupied or used only by young men.

Urban populations are becoming increasingly diverse, largely as a result of immigration. In some instances, this results in upheaval and conflict, particularly when newcomers compete with settled communities for scarce resources. This is often the case when displaced people or refugees flood into the cities of developing countries, during times of war or environmental disasters. Evidence from a variety of contexts suggests that women tend to play a constructive role in mediation and negotiation during times of social upheaval and discord at the community level.

However, urban communities can also be characterised by considerable social cohesion. This can be the result of a dynamic ethnic community spirit, or can be built up through developing a sense of community through community services, social support, and a bottom-up approach to community development. Here again, the participation of women is often depended upon, either explicitly, or by building on the existing strengths of women's organisation and networks at the neighbourhood level.

*Women-headed households*

A gender perspective shows that globally there is a growing diversity of family formations and household types. In addition to demographic factors, social and economic change have contributed to this. The industrialised countries have ageing populations, caused by the postponement of marriage and childbirth, while cities in developing countries are characterised by youthful populations. Everywhere there is a rise in single adult households and lone parent families, the majority headed by women. This has strong implications for housing outcomes.

It is estimated that globally one third of households are now women-headed, with the percentage often being higher in urban areas. Urban households headed by women are likely to be poorer than those headed by men. Women from these households engage in specific economic survival strategies to balance their role as sole income earners with that of running a household. For the most part, they do this alone, and face special problems when trying to engage in community life.

In Australia, the background paper prepared for the International Year of the Family estimated that a quarter of households are now headed by a sole parent, usually a woman. Of those living alone in single households, over 50 per cent were over 55 years of age, 70 per cent being women. While there was a 25 per cent increase in the number of all households between 1982 and 1992, the increase for single person households was 35 per cent (Cass, 1994).

In Canada in 1990, over two out of five unattached women (elderly and non-elderly combined) had incomes below Statistic Canada's "low income cut-offs" (usually referred to as the "poverty line"). Like the United States of America, the proportion of

```
┌─────────────────────────────────────────────────────────────────────┐
│                                                                       │
│   Inset 21.  Experimental housing and urban development, Germany      │
│                                                                       │
│       Within the framework of a research programme on Experimental    │
│   Housing and Urban Development commissioned by the Federal Building   │
│   Ministry in Germany, a research project was set up entitled          │
│   "Single Parents and Single Pregnant Women in Difficult              │
│   Circumstances". It addresses the problems such women have in         │
│   finding adequate accommodation. It seeks to understand the wide      │
│   variety of social and psychological pressures on many single        │
│   parents (85 per cent are women, of whom 3.5 per cent are pregnant)   │
│   which accumulate to disadvantage them in both the labour and the     │
│   housing markets. These include low incomes and discrimination in     │
│   the allocation of housing. The research also aims at identifying     │
│   ways of improving the supply of housing for single parents at        │
│   local level. One vehicle is to combine construction and social       │
│   measures in design and allocation of new and current housing         │
│   stock; another is to improve opportunities for access, such as       │
│   reducing discrimination and ensuring occupancy rights.               │
│                                                                       │
│   ─────────────────                                                   │
│                                                                       │
│   Source: National Report, Germany, OECD Conference on Women in the   │
│   City: Housing, Services and the Urban Environment, 4-6 October,     │
│   1994.                                                               │
│                                                                       │
└─────────────────────────────────────────────────────────────────────┘
```

Canadian single parents having children under the age of 18, whose incomes are below the poverty line is comparatively high in relation to European countries as a whole (Canada, National Report, 1994).

*Women-maintained families*

There is a growing awareness of the problems faced by women headed households and sole parent families. That they are increasingly a special target group for planners is a welcome step. However, it is important that the interests of women in need who are living in partnerships or alternative accommodation arrangements are not obscured. In developing countries there is evidence that women face enormous problems in the burgeoning numbers of women-maintained families, many of which include unemployed male partners and young adult sons.

According to the 1991 Census in Canada, the total population of 27.3 million lived in about 10 million households. Just over 3 million Canadian women were the primary financial maintainers of their households. This category, in turn, is a diverse group comprising lone parent families, families with unemployed men, and women who live alone (Canadian Mortgage and Housing Corporation, 1994).

The prevalence of women-maintained families illustrates the need for contemporary housing design, housing finance and urban planning not only to recognise the diversity in household composition and family formations and reformations, but also to take account of changes in the ways in which housing and the neighbourhood are used. Changes in production processes such as homeworking and increases in women's responsibility for household incomes, illustrate the need to respond to changes in workforce participation.

*Transitional or interim housing*

Homelessness is an increasing phenomenon in developed countries and according to national definitions, in Germany, the United Kingdom and France, more than one per cent of households are homeless, while there are at least 2.5 million known or visible homeless people in the European Union. The European Federation of National Organisations Working with the Homeless (FEANTSA) believes that the true level of homelessness in Europe may be 5 million. There is evidence of a growing number of women and children relative to men, becoming homeless (OECD Report on Housing and Social Integration; 1995).

Policies to address homelessness are concerned with prevention, reduction and rehabilitation. Thus for young women, reducing violence and abuse in the home and community constitutes an important preventive measure. Tenant protection measures are important in order to reduce the incidence of homelessness in the future. Rehabilitation of the homeless is often difficult, and depends on the availability of transitional or interim housing.

In the United States, for example, the Women's Centre of Rhode Island is a project supported by the US Department of Housing and Urban Development, which rehabilitates existing buildings to provide housing and supportive services to homeless women. "My Sister's Place Inc." is a project which has acquired, rehabilitated and manages transitional shelter facilities for young mothers and women with psychiatric illnesses. In Cleveland Ohio, Transitional Housing Inc provides transitional housing for homeless women and victims of domestic violence (National Report, United States, 1994).

*Housing for the elderly*

Particularly in the case of the industrialised countries, the issue of ageing populations is crucial in housing and planning for affordable and secure living environments. This is fundamentally a gender issue, as the majority of single person households are headed by elderly women. Moreover, age for women is often associated with poverty. Most of the current generation of elderly women, spent the majority of their adult lives as homemakers or in low-paying jobs. Thus they are often without adequate pensions or income security and find it difficult to maintain their independence. When they are widowed, elderly women are left with a huge gap in terms of finances, experience and knowledge. This particularly affects their ability to live independently as householders.

*Policy responses*

Housing and neighbourhood planning need to reflect the complexity of contemporary family life. Rarely are the needs of different households recognised in housing and

neighbourhood planning. The critical issue that has to be addressed in terms of housing is the growing mismatch between needs and provision, in terms of affordability, location and choice of housing types. For example:
- young women need access to transport and security to move around the city;
- women who are sole parents need affordable housing, proximity to jobs and services, child care and safety and security;

91

- women with adolescent children need facilities for this age group including access to public transport;
- older women need appropriate housing, access to services and maintenance assistance, proximity to family and safety and security.

### Improving the neighbourhood environment

Cities everywhere are faced with a policy dilemma associated with reconciling productivity objectives for the urban economy, and environmental improvement initiatives which are often costly.

The environmental problems of cities do not all occur, nor will they all be solved at the neighbourhood level. Neighbourhoods can play an important role in environmental improvement and management if they are treated as part of the city as a whole. Moreover, the neighbourhood environment is as important a component of human settlements as housing, and is vital for social cohesion and personal well-being. There are key gender dimensions involved, as women and men have different interests and needs in relation to the local environment and have different contributions to make towards its improvement.

### Green spaces, leisure and the neighbourhood

It is widely acknowledged in OECD countries that housing policies alone will not create liveable environments, nor will they tackle social problems in isolation. Thus a multi-sectoral approach to social renewal is increasingly favoured. Moreover, this is linked to environmental concerns which have reached a higher level of political and public awareness than in the past.

An environmentally aware, multi-sectoral approach includes creation of a residential environment which is free of physical, social or economic stress. Economic stress can result from high housing and transport costs, as well as unaffordable heating fuel. The latter will be considered in the following section. Social sources of stress result from loneliness and isolation, crime and lack of safety and security. These are also dealt with below. Physical stress can be caused by poor housing, noise, unsanitary facilities, lack of green spaces, leisure facilities and fresh air.

That lack of daylight and fresh air adversely affects people's health has been well documented (Grahn; 1994). It follows that neighbourhoods need to include green spaces and outdoor leisure facilities. The outdoor environment is vital for the healthy development of children and young people. For example, researchers have shown that the grades of junior school pupils in the United States have been falling. A longitudinal study of the problem over the last twenty years has concluded that this is the result of insufficient attention having been paid to the significance of physical surroundings to learning ability (quoted in Grahn; 1994). This issue becomes a particular preoccupation for women in their role as mothers.

Adults too, and especially the elderly, need green areas such as parks, both for health and exercise, and for social pursuits. Studies suggest that green spaces need to be sufficiently large or secluded to be able to leave the noise, sights and smells of the city behind. This is particularly important for both women and men engaged in the workforce, who are involved either in long commutes and factory or office work, or who undertake paid work from home. In the latter case, houses can become associated with work rather than rest and leisure, making communal space dedicated to leisure and play more important than ever.

The issue of safety in public spaces has become an increasing preoccupation of planners in recent years. This has largely been at the behest of women who have persistently put the issue on the agenda. Open spaces such as streets have lost their social function and are mainly traffic routes rather than places where people meet. Women often feel safe only in protected public spaces such as shopping malls. This provides a strong rationale for designing women- and children-friendly parks and leisure facilities.

Public space needs to be designed in a way that takes into account gender sensitive criteria of safety needs. Green spaces and parks should be multi-functional to meet the needs of socially diverse populations, and to combine different functions. Traffic, for example, can be reduced, particularly at certain times of day when children are playing. Space can be divided between playing fields, places to sit, and places to walk or cycle. Young mothers with babies and small children need to be able to chat and play without being disturbed by the more boisterous games of older boys, or without being fearful of interference by other adults. The Coram Fields Park in London has catered for this need by refusing entrance to adults unless accompanied by children!

*Home energy and the urban environment*

The use of energy in homes, particularly in countries of the North, accounts for a significant proportion of atmospheric pollutants, largely a result of inefficient and excessive use of domestic fuels. Clearly, although women should be key partners in any attempt to reduce energy consumption, this is rarely the case.

A recent survey carried out in Leicester, Britain's "first Environment City", found that women are the major consumers of domestic energy, and 68 per cent of those questioned took responsibility for household budgets. The issue of fuel poverty, where households are unable to afford the cost of energy to efficiently heat their homes disproportionately, affects women. Elderly people and children are particularly vulnerable to the consequences of poorly heated and ventilated homes. Thus the impact on women's lives and on their dependents, of expensively heated and poorly ventilated homes is considerable (Gunn-Peim and Branson, 1994).

*Leicester's home energy strategy*

Leicester is a multi-cultural city of 272 000, where diverse needs and expectations have to be considered in the context of a declining industrial base. Unemployment is currently 14.5 per cent. The city has 114 500 housing units, 29 000 of which are publicly owned, 5 500 under Housing Association ownership and 70 000 owner occupied. Fluctuating interest rates and high levels of unemployment have resulted in high housing costs for many families; a situation compounded by the high cost of domestic energy and homes that are expensive to heat.

## Inset 24. Leicester's home energy strategy, United Kingdom

### Objectives

- To reduce the consumption of non-renewable energy.
- To enable all citizens to have access to affordable warmth and a healthy environment.
- To provide a practical example of the implementation of Local Agenda 21.

### Operational Objective

- To enable every household in Leicester to take steps.
- To make their home energy efficient and to create a healthy environment in which to live.

### Benefits of the Home Energy Strategy

**Social:**

- Affordable Warmth;
- Thermal Comfort;
- Improved Health.

**Economic:**

- Job Creation;
- Training Opportunities;
- New Markets;
- Higher Disposable Incomes;
- Landlord Benefits.

### Environmental

**Local:**

- Improved Air Quality;
- Raised Public Awareness;
- Local Agenda 21.

**Global:**

- Greenhouse Effect.

---

*Source:* Gunn-Peim D., Leicester City Council Housing Department, A Home Energy Strategy for Leicester, September 1994. (1994) paper presented to the OECD Conference on Women in the City: Housing, Services and the Urban Environment, 4-6 October 1994.

As part of its Urban Regeneration Strategy, Leicester City Council provides means tested grants to increase energy efficiency and ventilation measures, to ensure affordable warmth and a healthy household environment. In order to reduce consumption of non-renewable energy and provide affordable warmth to all low income households, the emphasis is on energy efficiency as well as affordability. The Home Energy Schedule includes loft insulation, cavity wall insulation, heat recovery fans, low energy light bulbs, draughtproofing, central heating boiler controls, thermostatic radiator valves, gas condensing boiler and double glazing to windows.

Leicester's approach is a multisectoral effort to improve the urban environment and address urban poverty. It involves local government, private business and community groups. Women outnumber men by 3 to 1 on consultative groups and their level of motivation is high. They express concern over unhealthy living environments and anxiety over the impact on their children's health. Partners in the Home Energy Strategy include citizens' groups, private sector companies, social services, health services, the education department and energy utility companies. An awareness of the gender issues involved, including those around participation of women in partnerships, are brought out in training.

## Health and safety in the city

It is important that in any multisectoral approach to urban development, health is included alongside other areas that make up urban affairs. Moreover, the link between urban poverty and health is well established.

In countries of the developing world, the proportion of the urban poor is increasing and their health problems are becoming more critical. These include high levels of traditional health problems indicated by high maternal, perinatal, infant and child mortality rates, as well as malnutrition and infectious diseases. However, according to Harpham (1994), there are also ''new'' health problems associated with urbanisation and industrialisation, such as cancers, hypertension, mental illness, problems of drug and alcohol use, sexually transmitted diseases (including AIDS), accidents (traffic and industrial) and violence.

While diseases associated with the West are manifesting themselves in developing cities in the industrialised countries, diseases previously confined to the Third World or the past, are reappearing due to urban poverty and the growing problem of homelessness. Everywhere the existence or threat of crime, violence and conflict is apparent. In the case of both health and safety, there are clear gender dimensions involved.

### Women's health in the city

Health, defined as physical, mental and social well-being, is determined by a broad range of social, environmental, economic and biological factors. An individual's health status is influenced by gender, age, ethnicity, disability, sexual orientation, socioeconomic status, location and the environment.

A gendered approach to health care starts from the premise that there are biological and social synergies between the health of children and that of their parents. Engendering health policy means addressing the health needs of both women and men at all stages of their life cycle. The particular health needs of women arise out of their biological role in reproduction, as well as their tasks and responsibilities within the gender division of labour within a particular socio-cultural context (Beall, 1995).

Addressing women's health is important because women have the following gender specific needs and problems:

- complex reproductive system;
- contraceptive needs;
- particular mental health problems;
- isolation;
- responsibility for family health;
- poverty, particularly single households and lone parents;
- violence.

Thus women have health needs not only as users of health services, but as carers themselves, in the home and in the community.

*Women and urban health in Glasgow*

Glasgow, a city with almost a million inhabitants and with high levels of unemployment, exhibits considerable social and economic deprivation. It is not surprising, therefore, that the health of Glaswegians is poor compared to that of the rest of Scotland. Within the city of Glasgow itself, there are marked differences in mortality from the most affluent areas to the most deprived. Women living in the most deprived areas have twice the premature mortality rate of those living in the most affluent areas. The main causes of premature death in women are not breast and cervical cancer, as is popularly believed, but rather heart disease and lung cancer (Laughlin S. and McIlwaine G., 1994).

Women in Glasgow experience many other health problems and, according to their own perceptions, mental health is the area they feel to be the greatest priority. For example, 40 per cent of women living in a deprived area of Glasgow reported feelings of anxiety and depression. Safety at home, at work and in the community is also an important health issue. The problem of domestic violence is extensive and is being increasingly recognised in the city. However, despite the fact that at least 20 000 women are likely to have been the victims of physical and mental violence in Glasgow, only 3 500 sought help from Women's Aid, with 30 per cent of this number being admitted to a refuge.

Glasgow is participating in the World Health Organisation's Healthy Cities initiative, which is aimed at creating a collaborative approach to urban health. As part of the Glasgow Healthy City Project, the Women's Health Working Group was formed, bringing together representatives of the main statutory organisations (local authorities, the health authority and universities) with representatives of voluntary and community groups. This group, which provided legitimacy for a new agenda for women's health, was able to build on a decade of ideas and work in the area. In 1992 the group produced a Women's Health Policy for Glasgow.

The policy document is viewed as a lever for organisational change and aims at improving the health and well-being of all women in Glasgow. The objectives of the policy are to promote investment in women's health and to encourage a social model of health which is participatory and multisectoral in approach, all within a strategic framework. The priority issues for women's health have been identified as:

- emotional and mental health;
- support for women as carers;

## Inset 25.   The Glasgow model for women's health, United Kingdom

**Objective 1**

To raise awareness about women's
health needs and an understanding
of a women's health perspective.

**Implementation**

- adoption of policy by statutory
  organisations;
- implementation groups within each
  organisation;
- awareness raising programme;
- consultation with communities
  and women's groups.

**Objective 2**

To introduce awareness into policy
and planning processes of statutory
and voluntary agencies.

**Implementation**

- purchasing criteria for women's health;
- women's mental health strategy;
- health needs of carers;
- Zero Tolerance Campaign (campaign
  against violence against women).

**Objective 3**

To ensure women's health needs
and a women's health perspective
are incorporated into the delivery
of all services.

**Implementation**

- improved child care and creche
  provision;
- women in sport initiative;
- young women in schools initiative;
- abused women – service protocols;
- heart disease audit.

**Objective 4**

To ensure the provision of services
and support specifically for women.

**Implementation**

- centre for women's health;
- model well-woman service;
- health promotion materials;
- Glasgow Women's Health Book.

*Source:* Laughlin S. and McIlwaine G., (1994), paper presented to the OECD Conference, Women in the City; Housing, Services and the Urban Environment, 4-6 october 1994.

- reproductive health;
- reduction in the incidence of disease;
- health and safety at work and home.

Thus the Glasgow Women's Health Policy advocates a consultative, participatory and inter-agency approach to help address the health problems of women in the city.


## Safer cities: gender issues in public safety

The issue of safety is one of greater and greater urgency as cities become more violent. Violence and public safety are clearly gender issues. Young boys face different sorts of pressure than young girls, for example from gangs, and are as often perpetrators of violence as victims of it. A problem especially although not exclusively for women, is the close relationship between vulnerability to physical attack and sexual abuse. Although violence against women is associated with the domestic sphere, lack of public safety is also an issue. It is such a problem in some industrialised cities, that it can prove as effective as purdah in restricting women's mobility. The relationship between the urban environment and women's safety is encapsulated in the following extract from the Canadian National Report (1994) for this Conference:

"... violence and the fear of violence prevents women from full and equal participation in the social life of their communities and threaten our understanding of what should be the democratic functioning of our society ... In all the various reports generated about 'women and safety' the argument emerges that municipal plans and policies must better integrate the concerns of women by asserting that there are important relationships between the built environment and social relations."

Canada has gone further than most countries in addressing the problem of safety for women, at both federal and local levels. Much of the material in this section is thus drawn from the Canadian experience.

A national survey of 12 300 women published in 1993 confirmed that violence against women is systematic and widespread throughout Canadian society and that it is grossly under-reported. While most violence occurs in the domestic arena, the survey also found widespread fear among women for their personal safety in public places and linked the fear of crime to specific aspects of the built environment (Wekerle, 1994).

The federal government has begun to devote public resources to programmes of prevention. Over the past two decades a range of initiatives have increased public awareness and community involvement. Local municipal-level Safe City projects, in partnership with women's organisations, have generated solutions for preventing violence against women. They share several features:

- support for advocacy groups that prevent violence against women;
- organisational structures that involve citizens in policy making;
- a focus on educating and empowering citizen groups to become the experts on urban safety.

Toronto's Safe City Programme with a mandate to focus on the prevention of violence against women has become a model for other Safe City Programmes (Wekerle, 1994). The measures they started with included:

- incorporating objectives on urban safety in the Official City Plan;
- publication of a design guidelines manual on urban safety to be used in the development review of new proposals;
- a new parking garage by-law requiring improved security features;
- attention to personal safety in parks and recreation centres;
- installation of new pedestrian-oriented street lights throughout the city;
- better services in city-owned housing projects;
- free self-defence courses for women in all city-owned recreation centres.

All major departments were involved in the work of implementing the Safe City Committee recommendations and as a result, city staff, politicians and citizens worked together to improve urban safety.

---

### Inset 26.  **METRAC Women's Safety Audit Guide, Canada**

METRAC (Metro Action Committee on Public Violence Against Women) has developed a Women's Safety Audit Guide which has been widely used within Canada and in other countries to enable women to be more aware of environmental features which make them feel unsafe.

The guide is a simple checklist to assess the safety of particular public and semi-public places. In Toronto it has been used to evaluate parks, bus stops, recreation centres, schools, university campuses, housing projects and the public transportation system in terms of safety. Items to be noted on the checklist include:

- attention to lighting;
- visibility to others;
- possible isolated entrapment areas;
- nearby land uses;
- impressions of maintenance of the area.

The guide is effective because it encourages ordinary citizens to make urban safety their concern and it acknowledges that "women know a lot that traditional experts don't know about the environment and how the design of it affects how safe women feel".

---

*Source:* METRAC Women's Safety Audit Guide, Toronto Metro Action Committee on Public Violence Against Women and Children, 1989.

## Inset 27.  **Safe neighbourhood initiatives, Canada**

The MTHA's Safe Neighbourhood Initiatives reflect the priorities of local communities. These are determined through regular meetings and discussions between residents, MTHA staff, police and service providers. In most communities problems are related to drug abuse and trafficking, vandalism and threats of physical violence.

Solutions for security problems vary by community but include:

- formation of community-based staff/tenant organisations;
- hiring of community development workers;
- arranging social and recreational events;
- improved surveillance by security personnel;
- improved lighting and visibility.

A recent evaluation of the SNI confirms the need for adequate resources and comprehensive strategies involving support from all levels within a housing organisation. It found that participating communities have benefited in tangible improvements in security and that community organisation has been fostered, with residents feeling empowered to work to solve community problems.

---

*Source:* Kiff-Macaluso, J., "Safe Neighbourhood Initiatives (SNI)", paper presented to OECD Conference on Women in the City: Housing, Services and the Urban Environment, Paris, 4-6 October, 1994.

In response to concerns by community-based women's groups that the focus of the Safe City Committee should be more broadly defined, a grant programme to support community-based strategies to prevent violence against women was established, supporting such programmes as:

- conflict resolution training for community-based agencies;
- young women's safety projects in community centres in low income neighbourhoods;
- educating health professionals serving minority communities on the issue of violence against women.

The Metropolitan Toronto Housing Authority (MTHA), has developed an effective programme for community participation in promoting security in public housing communities. The Safe Neighbourhood Initiatives (SNI), described below, have been used to reduce crime in eleven communities in the metropolitan area. Plans are underway to use the model in other public housing communities throughout Canada.

## *Safer homes: combating violence against women*

It has taken many years of active campaigning by women to get the issue of
violence, and particularly domestic violence, rated as a development issue. Domestic
relations have long been regarded as belonging to the private realm and not the concern
of policy makers and planners. However, there are a growing number of examples of
policy makers and planners beginning to confront the issue of domestic violence, and to
address it in policy and planning terms. For example, in many countries a process of
campaigning and advocacy work on the part of women's organisations has resulted in
changes in police training on the issue of domestic violence.

*Chapter 5*

# URBAN SERVICES RESPONSIVE TO DIVERSE NEEDS

"Functionally fragmented urban constellations have made it difficult for women to manage the tasks of daily life. Although women have played an active role in local government, they have left the 'hard' policy making, that is the decisions dealing with technical affairs and construction to men. Thus the system of representative democracy has not been able to meet the urban and environmental needs of children, youth, women and the elderly."

**Ms Sirpa Pietikäinen, Minister of the Environment, Finland and Chair of the Theme on Urban Services Responsive to the Needs of Women and Children, OECD Conference on Women in the City, Paris, 4-6 October 1994.**

It is widely recognised that there is an urgent imperative to improve urban design and services to make cities correspond better to human needs. The argument arising out of this Conference would make two further points. First it is important to disaggregate the concept of human needs because women and men use and experience the city in different ways. This has to be recognised and responded to by planners, not only for reasons of equity, but in the interests of effective urban development.

Second, the "social improvement" resulting from consultative, participatory and human-scale urban design and services may result in meeting ecological goals as well. For example, compact structures and multifunctional areas mean less travelling and traffic congestion, less energy consumption in general and less urban sprawl. The Conference felt it important that ways be sought, for example through transport policy, land use planning and zoning regulations, to change the urban environment in favour of people in the community.

**Accessibility and mobility in the city**

*Accessibility and mobility in the city: a question of space*

The particular difficulties faced by women in present urban environments in all OECD countries, are exemplified in a report on the Netherlands (L. de Ridder and

103

E.J. Modderman) presented to a Council of Europe seminar (Athens in 1990) on the Participation by Women in Decisions Concerning Regional and Environmental Planning (quoted in the OECD Conference Proposal, 1993):

The spatial division of functions (*i.e.* the concentration of houses, commercial activity, industries, recreation, etc. in separate locations) has been the credo in physical planning policy in the Netherlands for quite a time. Under the influence of the increase in scale, this split between living, working, and recreation has grown larger. Municipalities have been fused as were hospitals and schools; corner shops have been replaced by large supermarkets. This has led to important facilities being situated at ever greater distances from each other. The concept of the spatial division of functions was easily accepted as the concept of the family was strongly supported in the Netherlands. The man was regarded as the breadwinner in this model and as the central figure of the family. Attention was paid to movement between home and work but not to the everyday pattern of activities of housewives.

It is no longer realistic to take the traditional family unit as the starting point for physical planning. Whereas the number of women in paid employment was a mere 22 per cent of the labour force in 1960, that percentage has risen to 38 per cent which shows that women cannot be regarded as only housewives. Furthermore, "traditional" families nowadays constitute less than 50 per cent of the number of households in the Netherlands. The proportion of non-family households is on the increase. The number of single-person households has risen from 12 per cent to 22 per cent in 1981. The influence of shorter working hours has contributed to women and men wanting to combine more tasks during any one day. The present spatial structure is a hindrance to this. The large distances which must be covered mean loss of time.

The Conference provided excellent examples of how "people-centred" planners with a gender perspective are confronting these changes. In Australia, for example, planners are looking at ways to create a more human scale in Australian cities, in which people can more easily travel to work, access services, and go about their daily lives. In Germany, ideas are being explored around the idea of "the city of short journeys". Behind this notion, lie three main ideas:
- compact settlement structures;
- multifunctional areas; and
- better spatial arrangements for living, working, shopping and leisure infrastructure.

The idea is to reduce travelling between work and other activities and to regain streets and open spaces as public spaces with social functions, and to induce a feeling of community control and a greater sense of cohesiveness and security. This turns on its head traditional urban planning philosophy which separated functions, keeping apart residential, commercial, industrial and even leisure areas.

## Accessibility and mobility in the city: a question of time

In a paper entitled "A Womanfriendly City: Policies Concerning the Organisation of Time in Italian Cities" (1994), Professor Carmen Belloni of Italy provided the Conference with an interesting example of urban planning based on consideration of time rather than space. The initiative arose out of the problem of cities being dysfunctional, and a recognition that deficient urban infrastructure was penalising particular sectors of the population, notably women. A law was approved in Italy in 1990 which provided the policy framework within which local administrations could pass new measures. These aimed at making the relationship between the city and citizens more user-friendly, and more directly related to daily life. It is no coincidence that prominent among the politicians and public administrators who concerned themselves with these issues were women.

The movement that sprang up around and elaborated these ideas was radically innovative in its analysis. Traditionally urban development has been governed by a spatial perspective, or a rigid Taylorist-Fordist division of time, based on prioritising work and production before all other public and private time. The innovative proposal for the reorganisation of urban life was centred around the concept of flexibility, not only in terms of space, such as the creation of multifunctional structures and areas, but in terms of the organisation of time. It was argued that the fixed rhythms and pace of urban life, constrained people. Reference was made to women in particular who, within the course of a day, a week or over a lifecycle, constantly have to balance multiple responsibilities.

The 1990 law in general sanctioned some principles of local autonomy, but also contained an article on the co-ordination of urban times. This was not enforceable, but was taken up by progressive cities or municipalities where women were organised. Implementation progressed in two main directions. The first involved a study of city timetables, including individual and family social time, and subsequently acting on these findings.

A national time-use survey was carried out by the National Statistics Institute (1993) using time budgets and introducing the gender variable. It was found that the greatest proportion of time (and of resources and energy) was spent on reproductive work, maintaining individuals and family members. This included domestic work, shopping, dealing with household administration and bureaucratic procedures, taking care of children, the elderly and the sick. This mass of socially important but largely hidden work, although quantitatively greater than paid, more visible work, was found to be the object of public policies only to a minimal extent.

Another important consideration highlighted by the research, was that the burden of daily reproductive work which makes possible the survival of individuals and families, is primarily borne by adult women, who act as links or liaison between private organisation and public, collective organisation of social life. This means that women either stay out of the labour market or seek work in jobs with shorter hours (typically in Italy the civil service or schools where pay and prestige are relatively low). Moreover, they are left with fewer opportunities for leisure, participation in public life and geographical mobility. Indeed the study confirmed that women are less mobile than men, travelling close to home (even choosing jobs on the basis of this criterion), and not in the evenings.

In some towns in Tuscany and Liguria, and in the City of Milan, Development Plans for Time were created, analogous to Urban Development Plans which regulate the use of space in the city. They were based on a preliminary analysis of the differentiated needs of the various sectors of the population. In some cases, information has been collected and co-ordinated in order to inform citizens of the complex co-ordination of cities' timetables and of how services operate. Various methods have been used from publishing manuals, to activating telephone help lines, to producing videos. In some cities, political bodies with the name of Times Councils, have been set up to provide the machinery to deal with negotiations between different social groups concerning proposals for modifying timetables.

With regard to local bureaucracies and the administrative services of cities themselves, it was found that opening hours were often problematic for families, as they were usually open to the public only for very short times, mainly during the mornings. Moreover, opening times for different services were not co-ordinated, requiring multiple journeys and absences from work (usually of the woman, as the family member with the less well paid and less important job). However, it was difficult to propose changes to shop opening hours for a number of reasons. Commerce is very fragmented in Italy, so measures were hard to introduce and enforce.

Traffic and mobility, especially in big cities, were found to be particularly problematic. Long journeys to work, usually by men in private cars, have negative effects on them, their families and the environment. On the other hand, women depend more on public transport which is inadequate and unreliable. Poor public transport marginalises and isolates women, so that improvements in traffic and transport enhance gender inclusiveness and citizens' rights generally.

Examples of practical measures to improve traffic and transport included introducing flexible school hours, building cycle tracks, reaching agreements with taxi-drivers to reduce, or subsidise fares in the evenings, for less accessible places or for those in high-risk areas.

The movement to understand daily lives and urban time in Italy also set out to tackle social policy issues, particularly those that would make the city more liveable for women-as-carers. For example, as far as babies and children are concerned, the daily hours and annual calendars of kindergartens can be increased. Baby-sitting services for the evening or short periods during the day can be organised. Games libraries and recreation centres for pre-school children and for after-school hours can be set up. Activities can be arranged for children during the school holidays. "Time banks" can be set up within parents' networks, through which members can exchange for child care.

For the elderly, strengthening medical assistance and transport facilities to hospitals and health centres can reduce their dependence on other family members. Home assistance (for example cleaning and shopping) for independent but frail old people can have the same effect. Recreational and entertainment centres for the elderly can provide them with alternative social networks.

Initial attempts to implement the law have had both positive and negative effects. On the positive side, the attention which this approach has drawn to the unequal distribution of work in the management of day-to-day life in the city has encouraged a proliferation of studies and surveys on daily life in the city. These have concentrated on women. It has also put the spotlight on the quality and organisation of services in the city and the adequacy of architectural and urban design factors. The process itself has also led to close collaborative efforts and has enhanced a multisectoral approach to urban development. Within urban public services, there has been a process of reflection on the organisation of work and on the need to retrain staff. Some institutions have gone so far as to run training courses on the planning of urban times and urban timetables, and an Urban Time Planning Association with gender sensitive goals and statutes has been formed.

On the negative side, as something radically new, it has led in some cases to opposition and open conflict. Some employees and consumers who have so laboriously built into their lives mechanisms to deal with the ''jigsaw puzzle of multiple times'' in the city resent changes which upset personal organisation and family routines. Moreover, there is a conflict between women as users of services or consumers who demand greater efficiency and flexibility, and women as workers (for example in shops, schools or in the civil service). The latter frequently chose their work because of limited working days, and are reluctant to work longer or different hours outside their customary routine. The complex web of interests which goes to make up the organisational structure of the city emphasises the fact that women, like men, are not a homogenous category, and that the urban reorganisation which also achieves social equality cannot be achieved by rationalisation and linear approaches alone.

## *The gender dimensions of urban transport*

Studies on women's mobility patterns show that they differ greatly from men's. Women tend to work nearer their homes so they can reconcile work activities and family life. This restricts their choice of job. Men often spend more time travelling and are subject to stress from commuting.

There are also gender differences in the means of transport used by women and men. In France, sixty per cent of men outside the Paris region travel only by car. Everywhere, fewer women than men own or use cars. In Sweden for example, some seventy per cent of cars are owned by men. It is not surprising, therefore, that transport policies have been in favour of the car to the detriment of public transport, cycling and walking. Decisions about transport policy are taken by men ''in the prime of life''. These are the men who mainly use the private car (Duchène, 1994).

Everywhere, women are more reliant on public transport systems than men and seem to be more in favour of it. In France, for example, men only use public transport for ten per cent of their journeys, while two thirds of public transport users are women (Duchène, 1994). And yet even with regard to public transport, women's needs are often overlooked because of the focus on mobility rather than accessibility, and because of the preoccupation with the man's journey to work. In France, local public transport undertakings are mainly trying to attract more male passengers by emphasising speed and automation. At the same time they are losing women's custom because they ignore their priorities. If this form of transport is to be a real alternative, it has to better meet women's needs.

Working women who are trying to balance a job with domestic responsibilities and child care appreciate time gains and low cost of public transport, but more importantly, they need reliability as they have very tight schedules. Of female respondents to a recent Paris Transport Authority survey, seventy seven per cent complained about frequent malfunctions of transport services in Paris which disrupted their own timetables (Duchène, 1994).

As women usually remain responsible for household work, for childcare and care of the elderly and infirm, even when they are employed, they usually have more complex journey patterns than men. Women's travel needs frequently require transport outside of peak hours, and to alternative destinations from those of men, for example shops and markets, schools and clinics. Yet cost cutting inevitably involves a reduction in off-peak services, a consequence of the economic evaluation made by planners who use conventional cost-benefit measures which ignore social impact and place little value on the journeys women make in the context of their reproductive responsibilities.

As mothers and carers, women frequently have to escort others (children, the elderly, sick and disabled relatives and friends) and are often burdened with heavy or awkward loads such as shopping bags and pushchairs. These factors are not always accommodated by bus design or the "strap-hanging" patterns of above-ground or underground train transport. In the Paris Transport Authority survey, 81 per cent of women respondents said that public transport facilities are not designed for passengers who have things or children to carry (Duchène, 1994). A recent study in Tokyo reported that in one commuting station there were so many stairs that the energy spent climbing them was equivalent to ascending the stairs of a six storey building (Matsukawa, 1994).

Because of reasons such as these, as well as for economy, many women tend to walk when they can. The needs of pedestrians are often neglected by planners. This becomes a gender issue, as was pointed out by a delegate from Vienna, where two-thirds of pedestrians are women. They are constrained by time and space, and are the weakest group when it comes to policy issues around mobility. Women pedestrians in particular, benefit from wider and smoother pavements, shallower curbs and more and safer cycle ways and footpaths. The safety issue is also of growing concern with regard to public transport. Just as women pedestrians avoid unlit streets, isolated footpaths and dim underpasses, they also avoid certain forms of transport or destinations. They try to travel at certain times of day, or avoid travelling at all for fear of violence or harassment.

### Accessing retailing facilities

Availability of local shopping facilities and town centres easily accessed by public transport or pedestrians is a crucial issue for those without cars. The trend in many OECD countries has been to give more and more planning permissions for suburban shopping centres, or superstores and warehouses on city peripheries, which mainly serve people with cars. This in turn has led, in the minds of many, to the demise of local retail outlets and town centres, thereby inconveniencing the lives of many women who relied on these shops. Moreover, the prices of many consumer goods are cheaper in out-of-town hypermarkets, so that this "benefit to consumers" is not equally distributed across society (Takmaz Nisancioglu, 1994).

Thus the entire organisation of retail and wholesale distribution systems has a social impact which is gendered in its effect. The process of economic or commercial concentration towards larger and larger units, centred around the peripheries of towns, may also have an impact on the kind of employment which is generated, and on who has access to those jobs. This too would discriminate against the less mobile. The organisation of retail distribution systems also has implications for carbon dioxide emissions and the environment. Thus while current systems might appear to be economically and environmentally efficient in the short term, they may actually create social, economic environmental impacts which are destructive in the longer term.

The second issue in relation to retail facilities is the actual design and layout of shops and shopping areas. They are often not designed to cater for the needs of women, particularly those with children or disabled relatives. Mobility in and around shops is

---

Inset 29. **Accessing retail facilities: open sesame project, Haringey, United Kingdom**

Open Sesame is a unique project from a planning point of view, which specifically addresses the needs of women. It is also unique in the sense that it seeks active involvement of the community in bringing about positive changes to the built environment in the London borough of Haringey.

Given that women are more likely to rely on local shopping facilities and town centres which can easily be reached by public transport or by foot, the project focused on access problems in such commercial areas. The aims of the Open Sesame Project are:

- to highlight the access problems of women as carers and to raise awareness of planners and shop-owners on this issue;
- to encourage the business community to address the problems of access by giving awards to shops which improve access and facilities;
- to involve women living in Haringey in all aspects of environmental improvements.

Various women's groups participated in the planning and implementation of the project and together with the Council's Women's Issues Officer, organised two action days where women with baby buggies and shopping bags or wheelchairs surveyed the shops in terms of accessibility. A third action day was arranged for male planners who repeated the exercise, to experience the difficulties at first hand.

Open Sesame received widespread local and national publicity and thus achieved its aim of highlighting the access problem and of raising the awareness of planners.

---

*Source:* Takmaz Nisancioglu S., ''Accessing Retail Facilities: Open Sesame Project'', paper presented to OECD Conference on Women in the City: Housing, Services and the Urban Environment, Paris, 4-6 October, 1994.

therefore restricted. Shop entrances, circulation areas and lifts are often not wide enough for a wheelchair or double buggy to pass through. Ramps, or seating facilities for people to meet friends do not always feature in shops or town centres.

Toilets are also restricted and often do not provide space for breast-feeding mothers, or facilities for women to change their babies. Interestingly, this is not just a women's issue. There have been demands from fathers undertaking child care responsibilities that male toilets should also have baby changing facilities. Other demands that parents make are for shoppers' creches to be provided for children to be looked after for short periods.

It is not always the fault of planners who often face strong opposition from developers when requiring such facilities, and yet, if such facilities are built into the original design of buildings, they are cheaper and easier to provide. The objection appears to be that wider circulation spaces, more toilets, and so on, reduce the "selling area". In the United Kingdom, for example, apart from the provision of toilets in new buildings for people with disabilities, there is nothing in the Planning Legislation or Government Guidelines to encourage or oblige developers to provide other facilities.

## Employment and business in cities and neighbourhoods

As pointed out in the OECD's report on "Shaping Structural Change: The Role of Women" (1991), "an active society demands a new perspective on women as economic actors". Women's labour force participation is generally on the increase. In France, the massive entry of women into the labour market over recent decades means that today they represent 44 per cent of the labour force. For women it means that 77 per cent of those between the age of 25 and 49 work. These figures are particularly staggering when it is borne in mind that unlike other industrialised countries such as Britain, part-time work is not common (Nivard, 1994).

Women have entered or re-entered the labour market for different reasons at different times or depending on their personal circumstances. For example, many women were encouraged to take on jobs during the Second World War and were reluctant thereafter to return to the home to make way for returning soldiers. Many women wish to work for their personal fulfilment or to feel socially useful. Others take up employment to avoid the boredom and isolation of the domestic realm. For many women, however, engaging in paid work is not a matter of choice. During recent years real incomes have fallen in many countries of the world, making the contribution of women to household income crucial. For the large and growing number of single women and lone parent households, women are the only breadwinners.

In OECD countries, unemployment levels are around eight per cent, affecting 35 million people. The causes of unemployment often comprise a complex web of structural, economic, social, personal and environmental conditions. It is unlikely that economic development is going to provide "full employment" for a long time, so there is an imperative for urban planning to support economic development which breaks down barriers to job creation, self-employment and business promotion, and which provides flexible income earning opportunities and services for unemployed women and men and for local employers.

*Women and the urban economy*

In the formal urban economy, women are usually found in the service sector and in certain branches of manufacturing industry. In many regions there is evidence of female-led industrialisation, particularly in the context of export-led growth. However, women workers often experience insecurity and are concentrated in those branches of manufacturing industry which are the most labour intensive and the lowest paid, such as garments and textiles, food processing and electronics. In other instances, there has been a decline in women's labour force participation, particularly where the trend has been towards capital intensive production (Kusel, 1992). In relation to formal employment then, women are a legitimate focus of policy in that at present, they have fewer opportunities than men to acquire skills; they have less time and capacity to organise due to multiple demands on their energy and time, and because currently both legislation and cultural and gender stereotyping confines them to certain jobs.

Thus women's incorporation into formal employment is diverse and context specific. Moreover, a dualistic approach which distinguishes the formal from the informal economy is increasingly redundant. Today there is less homogeneity in the organisation of production globally, with a growing trend towards flexible specialisation, home-working and "cottage shop" firms. Increasingly the spatial separation between work community and domestic life is less obvious in many cities. Universally women are over-represented in the non-conventional labour force; be it dependent production such as piece work and sub-contracted home-working, or self-employment in small-scale production, petty trading and service provision. Formal sector firms are becoming leaner and more flexible, by cutting overheads, shedding jobs and sub-contracting parts of their operations to smaller units where fixed costs are generally lower and the proportion of women who engage in small-scale income earning activities has increased faster than that of men (Beall and Davila, 1993).

For many women working from home offers them an opportunity to combine domestic and community responsibilities with the need to earn an income, and can give them greater control over the labour process than production-line factory work. However, the utilisation of family relationships by employers and contractors is creating a new division of labour and is appropriating household space for production, trading or service activities. This can lead to additional stresses on households, particularly if the wider urban environment makes no provision for leisure and recreational pursuits.

Thus in relation to the urban economy, women remain a legitimate focus of policy, not only in terms of employment legislation but in terms of urban planning as well. This is by virtue of their location in a segmented labour market and the increasing feminisation of labour, accompanied by moves towards part-time and temporary or insecure employment. It is also justified by virtue of women's role in self-employment and small scale income generating activities, often in the informal economy. However, women and men are never just workers but have other social roles in the household and community which impinge on the manner and extent to which they engage in productive activities. Because women continue to be the primary carers in families and neighbourhoods, and the ones with greatest responsibility for household work and management, they require flexibility

> ## Inset 30.   Family and employment: Updating the gender contract, OECD
>
> More women – and also more men – are facing dual and often conflicting labour market and family responsibilities. Ensuring the compatibility of employment and family commitments within individual lives is a major challenge emerging from the process of structural change.
>
> ### The "social contract" and gender
>
> Life is organised around an implicit "Social Contract". Its two components, the gender contract and the employment contract define the current division of family and labour market roles. Within the gender contract, women assume the bulk of family care and domestic functions, while men are ascribed primary responsibility for the family's economic or financial well-being. The employment contract reinforces this division of labour by defining as its norm the sole breadwinner in continuous full-time lifelong employment.
>
> The social contract conflicts with the new reality of men's and women's lives. Dual earner and single adult families are increasingly common while households with full time homemakers have declined dramatically. Female labour market participation has multiplied in response to women's high employment aspirations, the economic needs of families and demands from the economy for more labour. Most women are now forced to juggle household and family demands with involvement in paid work structures designed to fit male employment patterns. Men miss out on the emotional rewards of the care and development of children because they are similarly constrained by the gender-based division of household and employment responsibilities.
>
> ---
>
> *Source:* OECD (1991), "Shaping Structural Change, The Role of Women".

in working time, career breaks to accommodate child-bearing and child-rearing, as well as the social infrastructure to make balancing their reproductive and productive roles more manageable.

## *The rise of women entrepreneurs*

The past decade has witnessed a rise in the number of women starting their own businesses. This not only increases the number of women entrepreneurs, but has the potential for creating jobs for other women. In developing countries, women have long been represented in the so-called informal sector. For some, what starts out as necessity, given their frequent exclusion from formal sector wage employment, turns into the opportunity to develop profitable micro and small-scale enterprises. Their success depends not only on their own acumen and capacity, as well as the household and social infrastructure they have to support them, but also on commercial and financial support.

There are growing numbers of women entrepreneurs. Personal circumstances are often the driving force behind women's decision to go into business, related to their failure to find paid work after a long period of job-hunting, their inability to balance their domestic responsibilities with inflexible working hours, or to a good idea worth testing in the marketplace. However, women can also choose to start their own businesses as a result of discontent with the workplace; low pay, inflexible working conditions, men being promoted in favour of women, and lack of career prospects.

There is an argument that the growth of women's firms can change entrepreneurial culture. Case studies presented in the OECD Newsletter Innovation and Employment (1993) suggest that "there is a special feminine culture of entrepreneurship: highly aware of their special needs and of the needs of their society, oriented to providing services that answer a previously unrecognised market demand, open to partnerships and very cautious". As old ways of doing business are challenged by social and economic change, it is possible that trends and practices in women's businesses will become more generalised and will create new responses and possibilities to economies coping with unemployment.

---

### Inset 31.  **Women's World Banking**

Women's World Banking (WWB) is an international, non-profit financial institution for women wishing to start a business. It was established in 1979 and has its headquarters in New York with affiliates in 40 countries throughout the world. It believes women need access to capital not grants, and it has a 95 per cent recovery rate on its loans. These are given directly or are facilitated through traditional banks. Traditional banks are not used to dealing with women's enterprises which are often considered too small and too risky to be creditworthy, so WWB plays an important educative role in showing that they are ignoring an important market niche.

In addition to banking, WWB facilitates networking, on-the-job training schemes, best practice exchanges, marketing and export networks. It also has an institutional development goal, working to build stronger local capacity in countries where the special needs of women entrepreneurs are ignored or poorly addressed. WWB President Nancy Barry says the main goal of the organisation is to "expand the economic participation of millions of poor women entrepreneurs, through direct innovative instruments, new relationships and effective systems which give poor women entrepreneurs access to banking services, markets and information".

*Source:* OECD Newsletter of the Local Economic and Employment Development (LEED) Programme Innovation and Employment, No. 14, December 1993.

*Improving education and employment opportunities for women*

In a context of high levels of unemployment, there is often resistance by some policy makers and planners to encouraging women to seek employment. However, growing numbers of families are women-maintained, women-headed households are increasing in proportion, and in joint households, women's incomes are often vital to family well-being or survival. Thus there is an imperative to imaginatively address the issue of employment for women. An example of a successful strategy which has both facilitated women workers and encouraged employment creation is the "Retravailler" (return to work) project in France. It was created as early as the 1970s to provide women a transitional period between family and professional life. During this time they could devote themselves to reorientation, updating, reskilling and decision-making with regard to career options and choices (Nivard, 1994). In the twenty or so years of its operation which has involved a wide range of employers, not only have women been facilitated as income earners, but new jobs have been created and the working time has been reduced or made more flexible. The project has made an important contribution, but continues to have a vital on-going task because women continue to make up over half the long-term unemployed, and women's jobs are often the most precarious and insecure. "Retravailler" also provides assistance to help set up similar organisations in other countries.

An example of employment creation at the neighbourhood level is provided by the Minneapolis Neighbourhood Employment Network (NET) (Brinda, 1994). For over a decade the Network has been helping residents of Minneapolis, Minnesota to find and keep jobs close to home. It is a long-term, integrated, community-based approach which is providing an example to other cities in the United States and beyond.

In April 1981 The Minneapolis Employment Strategy Task Force grew out of an initiative of the then Mayor Donald Fraser. It comprised business and community leaders, mandated to develop a strategy to enable "hard-to-employ" residents to share in the benefits of the city's planned economic development. The Task Force assumed that new job opportunities would continue to grow, that public sector resources would continue to decrease and that support services existed but access to them by the hard-to-employ was uncoordinated. They sought, therefore, to find more effective ways of utilising and integrating existing programmes and services.

The NET strategy was implemented from 1982. It was not just about helping people find jobs, but about helping to break down the barriers to productive, successful employment in cities today. An analysis of the characteristics of NET's diverse clients showed that most were between the age of 22 and 39 (although the range was from 16 to 62). They were about evenly divided between women and men, with large representations of Black, American Indian and White people. Fort-two per cent of NET users had children and 24 per cent were single parents. A number of NET clients had special needs such as learning difficulties or health and education problems.

The barriers to productive and successful employment ranged from illiteracy to a lack of reliable transportation; from low skills and self-esteem, to lack of child care; from family problems to lack of information about where to find jobs. Such diverse barriers required a long-term and flexible approach and the Task Force divided the city into a number of geographic units in order to identify and co-ordinate local needs, employers and support services.

NET's success and longevity is based not only on its innovative and timely response to client needs, but to the partnership approach it has at community level as well. Business-neighbourhood collaboration to improve employment opportunities has been fostered. This has provided employers with trained employees. Individual communities have been revitalised and stabilised.

NET specifically seeks to meet the challenges of helping women enter the work force in both traditional and non-traditional jobs through education and programme innovation. They have had projects to assist women in qualifying for non-traditional jobs such as fire protection and law enforcement. During 1993 the Job Bank affiliate of NET assisted over 300 women in entering the work force by providing neighbourhood recruitment, counselling and access to support services such as childcare and transportation assistance.

An affiliated organisation called Women Venture, in conjunction with the building trades unions and a training institution, has developed a programme called Project Blueprint. This recruits women from the NET Job Banks who are interested in occupations in the building trades. They are provided training and facilitated in starting employment.

Despite NET's success with regard to assisting women, its Co-ordinator Michael Brinda has the following to say:

"While a number of 'special' programmes have been designed and implemented to help women enter the labour force, for most low income women many barriers remain. It is the consensus of thought among Minneapolis employment professionals that far and away the greatest barrier is the responsibility of childcare. A common thread for those women who have made the transition to employment outside the home has been a resource network that can provide job listings and a strong support system of family, friends or professional counsellors" (Brinda, 1994).

---

**Insert 33.  The European Urban Charter on Economic Development in Cities**

The European Urban Charter also places strong emphasis on local authority initiatives in stimulating urban economies and creating urban employment. Its chapter on Economic Development in Cities the Charter holds out as principles that:

- Local authorities should ensure the economic development of their communities.
- Economic and social development are inextricably linked.
- A town is economically and socially part of its surrounding region or hinterland.
- Economic growth and development depends upon an infrastructure adequate to produce, sustain and increase that growth.
- Collaboration between the private and public sectors is an important component in urban economic growth and development.

*Source:* Standing Conference of Local and Regional Authorities of Europe 1993, The European Urban Charter, Council of Europe Press.

---

The challenge everywhere is to promote urban economic development which is sensitive to changes in the productive and reproductive responsibilities of women and men, changes in domestic living arrangements, residential patterns and the gendered nature of income and work needs of citizens of cities and towns.

*Chapter 6*

# CONCLUSIONS

## Action proposals from the Round Table

In the course of the Round Table discussion, representatives of OECD Member governments identified the following actions to improve the role and contribution of women to urban policies:

1. Enhance the theme of **"citizenship"** to recognise women's right to participate fully in all spheres of activity in cities.

2. Improve the **representation and participation of women**, especially of elected officials, at all levels of public life, in decision-making bodies which affect urban policies, and in urban planning and related professions.

3. Develop and introduce the use of **time series gender-sensitive indicators** and targets for use in the formulation of urban policies, and for monitoring and improving the representation of women in public life and in decision-making bodies.

4. Establish and seek appropriate financing for **networks** at the local, regional, national and international level: to develop a policy research agenda; to improve the formulation of urban policy issues and responses from the viewpoint of women; to organise links between experts and grassroots movements, between different countries and regions, and between different levels of political representation. An important role of the networks would be to:
   • highlight and foster examples of innovative **urban projects** which demonstrate a gender-sensitive perspective.
   • organise **conferences and events** at international, national, regional and local level to disseminate the results of research and projects which demonstrate the role and contribution of women to urban policies.

5. Make better known, **via the media and new information technologies**, innovations in urban policy desired by women such as:
   • relating environmental and social issues to key urban policy sectors such as transport, housing and economic activity;
   • the development of a planning process and system of urban management which incorporates the views of the diverse groups making up the urban population;
   • the use of legislation on equality to improve urban planning legislation;
   • improving the role and contribution of consumers of public services;

## Inset 34.   EUROFEM – gender and human settlements network

### Background

Three important international conferences dealing with the women's perspective in urban policy and planning took place in Europe in 1994: "The challenges facing European society with the approach of the year 2000" organised by the Council of Europe in Örnsköldsvik, Sweden, "Emancipation as Related to Physical Planning, Housing and Mobility in Europe", arranged by the Netherlands Institute for Physical Planning and Housing, and the OECD High Level Conference "Women in the City". Also the preparations for the Second UN Conference on Human Settlements (Habitat II) deal with important issues for women.

Although women are a heterogeneous population, they share certain common aims, such as the desire to gain access both to the planning and decision-making processes as well as to a greater variety of alternative solutions in organising their daily living. Women give high priority to a supportive local infrastructure, which also meets the needs of children, young people, and the elderly. These solutions seek to interweave functions instead of separating them to improve accessibility to jobs, facilities and services, a well functioning system of public transport, social safety, a housing market with a variety of household and lifestyles, and green spaces for cultivation and recreation in cities.

The development of new approaches for urban, rural and environmental planning means that special attention must be paid to the conditions which enable women to participate. This may require changes in legislation, in organisation, and in the distribution of resources. The promotion of empowerment also requires the use of different strategies ranging from the micro to the macro level. The diversity of everyday life can be respected only if structural and mainstream solutions are simultaneously assessed from the grassroots perspective and *vice versa*.

Participants in the three conferences are eager to continue exploring gender aspects of policy. The first EuroFEM – *ad hoc* working meeting was held in Helsinki, 25-26 January 1995. The Finnish Minister of the Environment, Sirpa Pietikäinen, has set up a secretariat to co-ordinate the network for the first three-year period and an **International EuroFEM Congress will be hosted by the City of Hämeenlinna, Finland in 1998**.

### Purpose

The purpose of EuroFEM is to enhance equality, equity, joy and harmony in our living environments.

The goal of EuroFEM is to create a network, which provides supportive arenas for women to develop innovative, realisable and visible projects and policy proposals. This implies the creation of a methodology for the mobilisation of women towards improving the conditions of everyday life in human settlements.

The areas of action in EuroFEM include housing, environmental policy, regional/ spatial planning, urban governance, transport and mobility, work and local economy, decision making and politics, services, impact of technology, alternative energy solutions, educational training and information exchange.

*(continued on next page)*

*(continued)*

The geographical range of the network covers Western and Eastern European and OECD Member countries, not excluding good contacts with corresponding networks on other continents.

All levels of action ranging from local to international and global may be involved with special focus on the interconnections and mediating processes between the overlapping systems.

Strategies will stress the promotion of new and empowering ways of thinking and acting in various fields and highlight the importance of good examples which demonstrate the perspective of women.

Qualifications for acceptance as a EuroFEM project are based on the following criteria:

- the majority of those who initiate, implement or benefit from the project must be women, but men are also encouraged to join. It is desirable that participants represent differences of age, social class, ethnicity and geographical area. Children and youth should have a special place within the projects;
- the projects should be innovative and demonstrate visibly the different approach of women in both thinking and acting, Even if the projects are concrete, they should comprise a critical and self-reflective approach;
- the content of projects may vary. Central themes are regional and local planning, housing, urban governance, mobility, work and the local economy, services, energy, impacts of technology, culture and decision making. The common denominator is the ecological and social promotion of everyday life which transcends administrative and disciplinary boundaries;
- the range of projects may comprise both small and large ventures. There will be a special focus on projects which shed light on the interrelationships of the system or the impact of macro decisions on everyday life.

**Participation and organisation**

Participation is invited from women or networks which currently have or are planning to implement and evaluate a concrete project which fits the criteria described above. Projects in respective countries should be financially resourced but additional international funding may be sought.

A second ad hoc meeting took place in The Hague, Netherlands in May 1995 and the third ad hoc meeting will take place in 1996 in Italy.

**For more information contact:**

Ms. Irma Uuskallio        or       Dr. Liisa Horelli
Ministry of the Environment             Hopeasalmentie 21 B
P.O. Box 399                        FIN-00121 Helsinki
FIN-00570 Helsinki               FINLAND
FINLAND                        358-0-6848867
Tel. 358-0-19919347            358-0-68-45224
Fax. 358-0-19919380
Internet : Irma.Uuskallio@vyh.fi

- attributing greater importance to questions of everyday life in the making of urban policy;
- improving safety and combating violence in the home, in the street and in public places;
- promoting cultural and leisure activities and facilities which recognise and enhance the contribution to and role of women in society.
6. Ensure that **gender issues in urban policies** are taken into account:
    • in the UN Conference on Women in Beijing in 1995;
    • in the UN Habitat Conference in Istanbul in 1996;
    • in the urban policy agendas of all levels of government;
    • in the programmes of work of international organisations;
    • in educational institutions and by professional bodies in the urban policy and related fields.

In summary, the Round Table agreed that women should:
- participate;
- identify the pathways and opportunities to enhance participation;
- work for recognition of diversity in the community;
- create and participate in projects and secure the continuation of some of the ideas and networks formed during the OECD Conference on Women in the City.

During the Round Table Ms. Sirpa Pietikäinen, Minister of the Environment of Finland, proposed the creation of a EuroFEM Network to support and encourage women-led initiatives in human settlements (see Inset 34).

**Reports by rapporteurs of the conference themes**

*Theme I: Women and urban policies*
*Rapporteur: Ms Janet Kiff-Macaluso, Canada*

Theme I on **"Women and Urban Policies"** established an intellectual framework for the entire Conference. The issue papers presented were supported by illustrative case studies of innovative practice at the local level.

First the **historical context** was recalled, explaining how classical urban planning has placed women in a secondary role in urban development and tended to reinforce this position. Changes to the conception and processes of urban planning to bring it more into line with the evolving needs of today's citizens were seen to be long overdue. Speakers offered a number of policy solutions developed from a variety of perspectives. The view that cities no longer respond well to modern demands and that people with restricted access to resources are usually those who are most disadvantaged permeated the presentations and discussions. It was stressed that the majority of those with restricted access to resources tend to be women, particularly the elderly and middle-aged, as well as children.

There was a consensus that cities need to be recognised as dynamic structures. Continuing change – socio-economic, cultural and demographic – requires that **urban policies also be flexible and dynamic** if they are to respond well to the needs of city dwellers. For example, the focus of modern planning on the traditional family as the main economic unit of production is problematic in view of the increasing diversity of the composition of family groups and increasing numbers of people living alone.

It was stressed that the important changes occurring in cities affect women deeply. Women represent a high proportion of urban populations and must be a major focus of urban policies, planning and politics. However, caution should be exercised not to replicate the mistakes of our predecessors in the domain of urban planning, who developed cities on the concept of a modern, uniform man. It should be recognised that women are not one homogeneous group and future policy developments should take this fully into account. There are elderly women; working women; women with the majority of responsibilities in the domestic sphere; there are women who are trying to balance many of these roles at the same time.

The Conference also recognised that women are **not the only group** which has been excluded from urban governance, from the development of urban policies and from the planning of our cities. Other groups also suffer from discrimination and these too must be included in the planning process. Cities must be inclusive and welcome social diversity.

One possible way of examining and dealing with the diverse needs of residents of cities which has been put into operation in several Scandinavian countries, is to focus on the concept of the needs for "**everyday life**". Finland provided a good example of one way of doing this through the inclusion of children in the planning process at neighbourhood level. This is inclusive of **all people** who live in cities, and of their economic needs, their social needs and the requirements of the urban environment. This concept can also be sensitive to gender issues.

Theme I noted the **lack of information** available to assist in providing for the needs of different groups which make up the urban population. There is an urgent need for **gender-sensitive information** as well as information about other groups such as visible minorities, people with disabilities, the elderly and the young.

A main conclusion arising from this analysis of the dynamics of the city is that we need **new forms of governance.** In the past, planning has tended to be sectorally and hierarchically oriented and there is, perhaps, now a need to create **horizontal forms of organisation**, to have more co-operative policy making, and to include groups which are negatively affected by current policies in order to make urban policies more responsive to the needs and the aspirations of **all citizens.**

In the discussion, it was suggested that women's issues should be brought into the **mainstream** of politics and policy development. The advantages of such an approach are that this prevents the marginalisation that may occur when women's issues are regarded as a sector and are not substantially resourced as a result. By integrating women's issues into mainstream policy-making, greater control may be exercised over the resources which are directed towards specific needs. However, the discussion also raised concern about mainstreaming in as much as there could be a loss of influence as women's issues became one of many that have to be taken into consideration within policy development, and that the role of **grassroots movements** could be diminished.

It was argued that this need not happen as issues can be mainstreamed whilst maintaining a role for advocacy groups and having officers that particularly monitor the status of women to ensure that a reduction in priority of these issues does not occur. Norway provided a working model for integrating women's perspectives into the mainstream of the planning process, while recognising the need to continue the grassroots women's advocacy movement which has brought the issue of the needs and contributions of women to urban policies to the fore. A case study from Switzerland indicated some of the difficulties which are associated with improving the participation of women, whether it is at the grassroots or at a more formal level.

The need for women's issues to penetrate urban institutions through mainstreaming while maintaining local activism, highlighted the importance of **forging strong links** between the grassroots movement and professionals developing policies, as well as between those same professionals and the ultimate decision-makers. It is evident that the more women hold positions at all of these levels, the easier and stronger these links will be.

However, it was stressed on many occasions throughout the debate, that **increasing the number of women politicians** or the proportion of women entering the planning and related professions, **does not suffice**. Other tools can be used and other areas need improvement. What was highlighted was the need to train professionals, **both men and women**, so that they understand and can include women's perspectives within their professional frames of reference. This involves knowing how to gain the perspective of women and then using this information in planning and managing cities. This requires gender-sensitive, economic, social and health data, including better information networks and specific strategies which correspond to women's needs and facilitate the contribution which they can make.

Finally, in this Theme, it was understood that there is an **important role for the OECD to play** in setting priorities in the arenas of women's and urban affairs so that Member countries of the Organisation can begin to understand and ultimately respond. The OECD also has a major role in setting an example for how **new forms of governance** can be formulated and established and how the **mainstreaming** of women's issues can actually be achieved.


*Theme II: Housing and neighbourhood environments designed with women and children in mind*
*Rapporteur: Mr George Cavallier, France*

How does one go about describing the wealth of ideas that were exchanged on the theme of Housing and Neighbourhood Environments Designed with Women and Children in Mind during the Conference?

There were so many varied, interesting papers, some overlapping with other themes, that it would be hard to summarise all that was said.

So perhaps it would be better to adopt another approach and endeavour to pick out the most significant strands of the debate, the main points that recurred in the majority of papers.

This is the approach I have opted for. Without wishing to oversimplify – although that is the risk a rapporteur runs – I have divided my report on the debate into three convergent parts. The first is a statement on the consensus achieved on the objective; the second expresses the hope that what has so far been possible can now be achieved; and the final part outlines a possible thrust for future policy.

1.  **Unanimity on the objective: promoting the role of women in the design and management of housing and the urban environment is far more than just wishful thinking – it is a must.**

There are two distinct and mutually supportive reasons for this.

**First**, women suffer more than men from the inconvenience caused by poor housing design and the failures that stem from bad urban planning. Apart from the direct functional implications that such failures and defects can have, women are perhaps more than men the victims of the segregation that may result. They are highly sensitive, for example, to the feeling of being boxed in and isolated when specific forms of housing are located too far from city centres.

Changes in lifestyles (due to an ageing population, the increase in female employment, and the growing number of single parent families) can only aggravate these drawbacks.

So there is a good reason to eliminate such handicaps, close the gap and tailor housing and urban planning to the legitimate aspirations of women. This is the initial reason why we propose that policy should be designed **for women**.

The **second** reason, perhaps less obvious, raised less often but nonetheless important, is that women, by their very essence as much as by their role in society, possess a wealth of sensitivity, skills, knowledge and potential that should be mobilised for the benefit of all.

Yet in every country we have failed to put to good use the potential women have to enhance housing and the shape of our cities. It is therefore high time that we set to work, not only for women but also, and above all, **with women** for the benefit of all those living in the city.

2.  **One hope has emerged: new opportunities are arising, and it could be that what was formerly impossible may now be feasible. This is due not only to a change in attitudes but to the interplay of a number of objective factors.**

Apart from an undeniable increase in awareness of this issue, it would seem that the major economic and social changes now disrupting urban planning and development will also produce an environment more conducive to this kind of work for and with women.

Urban decision-making is bound to be deeply affected by the profound change in the economic environment.

For instance, the globalisation of production will mean increasing unpredictability; the rise in real interest rates will leave decision-makers less room for manoeuvre and make them increasingly aware of their inability to make forecasts, even in the medium-term.

Social factors too have just as strong an impact. For instance society is increasingly heterogeneous, established values are questioned, authority and sources of funding become dispersed, failures abound and there is a growing demand for security.

Accordingly the values that affect people's private lives, their individual understanding, their ethics as individual citizens are gradually replacing the deference formerly shown to those in positions of political authority or reputed to have technical expertise.

For instance, the trend is shifting away from decreeing – *a priori* and from the top down – that a project is in the public interest, and is moving towards a more procedural approach, involving a somewhat painful process of dialogue, discussion and conflicting expert opinion, where necessary but difficult trade-offs have to be struck between widely differing values.

This shift has strong implications for urban planning and development:

– as the same causes can no longer be relied upon to produce the same effects, the rationale behind urban development must be adapted and responsive. Flexibility is the answer. There must be on-going co-operation between decision-makers, designers and users so that the necessary adjustments can take place gradually;
– the "object-led urban planning" and dogmatic totalitarianism that predominated for so long are now things of the past. The key word now is "multi-sectoral". The study of interaction and system effects is becoming decisive.

Admittedly these changes have not been painless, but they do offer the opportunity of giving life and substance to local discussion and local public action.

Accordingly, the hope is that the untapped potential women represent in terms of social and cultural creativeness, know-how and experience can be mobilised more effectively to achieve better designed housing and cities which are more user-friendly.

### 3.    Some directions for future policy.

Most of the papers strongly underlined the fact that policy is essentially based on the dynamics of local initiatives, and on the active participation of women who are directly affected by a practical community project.

Local initiative is irreplaceable, and it is in every country's interest to promote it. It means encouraging anything constructive at grassroots level, adapting to local circumstances, fostering partnership and developing mediation. This will serve not only to build sound projects but also to foster and strengthen social ties. It is therefore all the more important in sensitive neighbourhoods facing a combination of problems and failures.

But local initiative has its limits and some pitfalls must be avoided:

– optimisation is only achieved when local initiatives are in line with national priorities and there is cross-fertilisation between action at every level. To be fully effective, the bottom-up approach should coincide and create synergy with top-down measures. Urban policies should ensure that the appropriate fora and arrangements are there to provide institutional opportunities for comparing, interfacing, combining and dovetailing the two approaches;

- defending local interests in an antagonistic or short-sighted way may lead to isolation and self-protection, failure to open up to the outside world, or beggar-thy-neighbour attitudes;
- local projects cannot rely solely on the energy and strength of local actors. They also require the support and participation of economic decision-makers with a direct influence on the project, even if they are based elsewhere;
- local initiatives are usually planned over the relatively short term, whereas structural policy for urban development can only bear fruit over a longer period.

Apart from this general thrust, a number of priorities emerged from the case studies and subsequent debate:

- In democracies such as ours, public awareness is the main factor, even the driving force, behind any far-reaching social change. Only by changing attitudes, ideas and patterns of thinking can scope be created for genuine reform. It is therefore essential to promote the role of women in the design and management of our everyday environment, to mobilise opinion and make people aware of the size and seriousness of the issues at stake.
- But awareness, however essential it may be, can never replace a detailed grasp of the issue. Better understanding will lead to more effective action. Observation of what is happening in our cities and neighbourhoods is highly inadequate and should be developed on a large scale. For instance, who would have thought, had we not been told by the Healthy Cities Project, that at least 20 000 women were victims of domestic physical or mental violence in Glasgow every year?
- Efforts must also be made to develop the tools linking facts or statistics to decision-making. Housing requires particular analysis, in terms of both demand and markets.
- At a time when society is growing more complex and the future less predictable, sound management means diversifying the housing supply as much as possible by acting on supply factors (type, size, location, type of funding, etc.) and matching it more closely to demand, which is in turn becoming increasingly diversified.
- Given the limited resources available to many female heads of households, and the obstacles they encounter in taking out loans, it is vital to eliminate discriminatory practices regarding access to loans, and to develop every means possible of helping them to remain creditworthy when they run into difficulties (identifying women with problems, helping them with formalities and procedures, setting up mutual guarantee or solidarity funds, providing help to prevent eviction, as well as supportive social services, etc.).
- Even if the democratic process is growing increasingly abstract, remote and purely relational, and even if the technical planners are losing sight of local realities, there is still considerable social communication thanks to urban public spaces. Streets, squares, parks and community facilities should remain places where people and ideas can circulate freely, where people can mix, mutually

acknowledge one another, harmonise their behaviour and learn what citizenship means. Particular attention should be paid to the design and management of these open spaces, which have been far too neglected recently. Experience has shown that when it comes to urban development, "empty" spaces are as important as "full" ones.

- Rising insecurity, the spread of petty crime and growing drug abuse are crucial issues when it comes to peace in our cities. Women, often the first victims, are particularly anxious about this. Government has a decisive role to play here. But the gap is widening between the growing demand for a secure environment and the lack of success achieved with repressive measures, which may well be essential but are proving singularly inadequate. Accordingly, the preventive approach, which has already proved its worth, should be systematically developed. Security should be treated as a public good, produced on a joint basis through preventive work that is interdisciplinary, pragmatic, co-ordinated, based on observation and dialogue, and mobilising actors at grassroots level with experience of the workings of self-regulation at local or community level.
- New information and communication technologies certainly hold out promising prospects. They can be put to good use in promoting women and their role in cities, particularly through the provision of special services delivered direct to the home. There have been convincing experiments to prove it. However, we should beware of the perverse effects; because a certain amount of skill and training is needed to operate these technologies, they may – if no conscious, deliberate policy is put in place – merely broaden existing divisions and heighten discrimination against women.
- Finally, to accelerate structural change and make these ideas a reality, it is vital that women not only participate in local initiatives as they are already doing, but also that they be given genuine responsibility, as much in public and political life as in the professional world of urban development.

## Theme III: Urban services responsive to the needs of women and children
### Rapporteur: Ms Maria de Lurdes Poeira, Portugal

The Chair of the Session, the Minister of the Environment, Finland, Ms Sirpa Pietikäinen, stressed three main points at the outset of the Theme on Urban Services Responsive to the Needs of Women and Children. First, the provision of urban services is a political and ideological issue concerning both the different everyday lifestyles and the different values of individuals; second, the majority of social questions are related to gender; and third, mobility issues are different as they relate to women and men.

The Theme focused on three aspects of urban services: Accessibility, Mobility and Improving Education and Employment Opportunities.

### Accessibility

Accessibility was analysed from two different perspectives. First, **physical accessibility**, and secondly **temporal accessibility or timing aspects**.

A case study on physical accessibility – the "Open Sesame" Project from Haringey in the United Kingdom – examined accessibility to shops and services and highlighted the importance of **location and design** for women, particularly those with children and/or elderly people. There was agreement that the search for efficient and effective solutions to improve access requires that **diverse groups of actors** be consulted in the development of projects: the users (mostly women); the planners; and the developers.

Next, an Italian case study concerning **new timetable arrangements** for urban workers aimed at facilitating accessibility to work and to the home demonstrated that the issue of the utilisation of time has great importance for women. This approach also requires the involvement of the diverse groups making up the urban population. The changes proposed must be efficient, must consider the issue of optimal location of services and, ultimately, the social impacts of any proposed solutions. Women are well placed to be involved in the formulation of new arrangements considering their important role in urban society and the institutional support they provide.

*Mobility*

Mobility is an essential aspect of high quality urban life which affects the lifestyle and opportunities of all residents. If transport provision does not take into account the needs of the different groups utilising the urban system, the city cannot be efficient, convenient or safe for everybody. This was stressed by the Japanese example which focused on the elderly as one of the vulnerable groups within urban society. Another example was the use of mobility indicators in France which showed that women are more affected by the negative consequences of the greater use of private cars and by the non-participative planning of the public transport system. The present crisis affecting urban systems, especially the economic and financial constraints, is having negative consequences on women's lives because of the limitations being imposed on the possible solutions for improving services such as much needed improvements to public transportation systems.

*Education and employment opportunities*

The third aspect of this theme focused on education and employment opportunities for women. The main issue relative to the improvement of the quality of life for women in cities was highlighted by the "Retravailler (return to work) Project" in France and by the Minneapolis Neighbourhood Employment Network Project. Education and employment are essential elements in improving the life of women in cities. However, there was agreement that solutions must be viewed cautiously. Many employment opportunities are short term solutions to longer term problems that require a much greater sustained effort. Many are also of an illusionary nature, in the sense that they are not well integrated into the socio-economic system of cities.

The presentations and discussions under the theme on Urban Services gave rise to a number of conclusions of a more general nature:

– First, **women are important urban actors** and must participate in the discussion, assessment and the decision-making process for the development of urban projects.

- Second, **information to facilitate analysis and assessment of urban issues must be made available** and women must, through improved education, information and/or by other specific mechanisms for action, attain sufficient capacity to allow them to analyse urban processes and propose solutions adapted to their specific perspective.
- Third, **participation and action** must be integrated into global proposals and processes aimed at achieving a more balanced urban system.
- Fourth, there is a need for urban planners to move forward **from defining problems to proposing innovative solutions** which are supportive of women.
- Fifth, numerous innovations and mechanisms which have been experimented with in developing countries under very difficult conditions have shown promising results. These set an example for OECD countries. **Exchange of information** is critical if innovations and improvements are to be made in the quality of life of women in cities of both OECD and non-Member countries.

**Conclusions of the Chair of the Conference, Ms Jean Augustine, M.P.**

The OECD Conference on Women in the City has provided a wide forum for consultation concerning the role of women in urban policies. Participants included national delegates, local officials, researchers, practitioners and representatives from international organisations, who came together to better understand the gender aspects of urban development and the role of urban issues in gender equality, and to deliberate on relationships with urban sustainability.

We started by drawing attention to the changing socio-economic and environment trends which are affecting cities and the people who live in them, in particular:
- globalisation of the economy and its implications at the urban level;
- high unemployment levels, often concentrated in certain areas;
- demographic changes, including ageing and changes in family structures;
- increasing awareness of the need to improve the environment and the local quality of life;
- increasing marginalisation of urban sub-groups and continued exclusion of these groups from urban decision-making.

Participants agreed that these deep economic and social trends require that urban governance and policies be rethought in order to respond better to the needs of the whole, heterogeneous urban population, and in particular to better reflect the gender aspects of urban development. To date, most action has been **ad hoc** or has consisted of pilot projects, implemented **on behalf of women**, where urban structures and services have been adapted to meet the needs of disadvantaged groups such as elderly women and single parents. It was stressed that too little has been done to plan and manage cities **with women.**

A fresh perspective is needed. Women should now be recognised as integral players in urban management processes. The involvement of women and men in the control of their everyday life will go far in improving gender equality. The new political and economic context must not exclude anyone from participation in urban affairs. Thus will require a spirit of dialogue and partnership.

The Conference participants were of the opinion that such a change and the resulting increased role of women in urban affairs will help to make the city function more efficiently and improve the quality of an urban environment that responds to the shared values of men, women and children.

Various initiatives that would help to **bring planning with women into reality** were identified during the Conference. It was stressed particularly that institutional and regulatory arrangements should be adjusted in order to enable women to participate more properly in the urban planning process. A number of positive actions should be undertaken:

– The social and physical environments of cities, and the economic efficiency of cities, require that the role of women and gender issues be integrated into the mainstream of the urban policies of governments.
– In particular, the role of women should be integrated into the mainstream of OECD activities. Projects in the work of the Group on Urban Affairs, including Cities and the Economy; Urban Governance (and particularly its indicators component); the Young and the City; and Distressed Urban Areas, clearly should integrate gender considerations. There should be a systematic follow-up to this Conference.
– Other OECD units also deal with sectors of urban affairs whose efficiency has gender dimensions (*e.g.* transportation, employment, environment, industrial practice and trade), and gender relationships should be systematically examined therein.
– OECD should build on current international initiatives concerning gender relationships in urban affairs by transmitting the results of this Conference for consideration in preparations for the Vienna Preparatory Conference for the UN Conference on women in Beijing; the Cities and the New Global Economy Conference; and Habitat II.
– The Group on Urban Affairs should consider establishing joint initiatives or networks with interested countries to deal with specific aspects of planning with women, such as housing, transport and local economic development.
– The Group on Urban Affairs should promote local experiments and transfer of experience in the area of women's participation in local planning and governance.

Finally, I urge all of you to transfer these conclusions to decision-makers in your own countries, and to follow through with actions. The delegates to the OECD Group on Urban Affairs should be encouraged to help the OECD and other bodies in their efforts to increase the role of women in urban affairs. I also urge countries which participated in this Conference to continue the dialogue and exchange which started at OECD during the last three days.

# References

BAUER, U. and KAIL E. (1994), "Design of a Housing Estate by Women: the 'Frauen-Werk' Stadt Project", paper presented to the OECD Conference on Women in the City: Housing, Services and the Urban Environment, Paris, 4-6 October.

BEALL, J.D. (1994), "Moving Towards the Gendered City", paper presented to the OECD Conference on Women in the City: Housing, Services and the Urban Environment, Paris, 4-6 October.

BEALL, J.D. (1992), "Integrating the Gender Variable into Urban Development" paper prepared for the Expert Group on Women in Development [DCD(92)], for the Development Assistance Committee of the OECD.

BEALL, J.D. (1993), "The Gender Dimensions of Urbanisation and Urban Poverty", paper prepared for the Division for the Advancement of Women, United Nations, for a Seminar on Women in Urban Areas, Santo Domingo, 8-12 November.

BEALL, J.D. et al., (1993), Social Safety Nets and Social Networks: Their Role in Poverty Alleviation in Pakistan, Volume II, Report for the ODA (UK) towards the World Bank Poverty Assessment for Pakistan.

BEALL, J.D. and DAVILA, J. (1994), "Integrating Gender into Policy for Manufacturing Industry", DPU Working Paper Series No. 66, October.

BEALL, J.D. and LEVY, C. (1994), "Moving Towards the Gendered City", paper prepared for UNCHS (Habitat) for the First Prepcom for Habitat II, Geneva, April.

BELLONI, C. (1994), "A Womanfriendly City: Policies Concerning the Organisation of Time in Italian Cities", paper presented to the OECD Conference on Women in the City: Housing, Services and the Urban Environment, Paris, 4-6 October.

BLAKE, H. (1994), "Women, the City and the Design of Utopia", paper presented to the Council of Europe Colloquy, the Challenges Facing European Society with the Approach of the Year 2000: Role and Representation of Women in Urban and Regional Planning Aiming at Sustainable Development, Ornskoldsvik, Sweden.

BRINDA, M. (1994), "The Minneapolis Neighbourhood Employment Network", paper presented to the OECD Conference on Women in the City: Housing, Services and the Urban Environment, Paris, 4-6 October.

Canada Mortgage and Housing Corporation. 1991, The Next Step: Interim Housing for Abused Women and Their Children.

CASS, B. (1994), "Accessing Affordable Housing", paper presented to the OECD Conference on Women in the City: Housing, Services and the Urban Environment, Paris, 4-6 October.

DOUGLAS, M (1992), "The Political Economy of Urban Poverty and Environmental Management in Asia: Access, Empowerment and Community Based Alternatives", Environment and Urbanisation, Vol. 4, No. 2, October.

DUCHENE, C. "Women and Urban Transport", paper presented to the OECD Conference on Women in the City: Housing, Services and the Urban Environment, Paris, 4-6 October.

GILBERT, A. and J. GUGLER (1992), Cities, Poverty and Development: Urbanisation in the Third World, 2nd edn., Oxford University Press, Oxford.

GILLIGAN, C. (1982), In a Different Voice, Harvard University Press, Cambridge, Manchester.

Glasgow Healthy City Project Women's Health Working Group (1994), Glasgow's Health, Women Count, Glasgow Healthy City Project.

GRAHN, P. (1994), "Green Structures – the importance for health of nature areas and parks", paper presented to the Council of Europe Colloquy, "The Challenges Facing European Society with the Approach of the Year 2000: Role and Representation of Women in Urban and Regional Planning Aiming at Sustainable Development", Ornskoldsvik, Sweden.

GREED, C. (1994), Women and Planning, Creating Gendered Realities, Routledge, London.

GUNN-PEIM, D., Leicester City Council Housing Department 1994, "A Home Energy Strategy for Leicester".

HARPHAM, T. (1994), "Cities and Health in the Third World" in D. Phillips and Y. Verhasselt (eds.), Health and Development, London, Routledge.

HEALEY, P. (1994), "Integrating the Concept of Social Diversity into Public Policy", paper presented to the OECD Conference on Women in the City: Housing, Services and the Urban Environment, Paris, 4-6 October.

HORELLI, L. (1994), "Children in the Design of Neighbourhoods of Cities, Finland", paper presented to the OECD Conference on Women in the City: Housing, Services and the Urban Environment, Paris, 4-6 October.

KIFF-MACALUSO, J. (1994), "Safe Neighbourhood Initiatives (SNI)", paper presented to the OECD Conference on Women in the City: Housing, Services and the Urban Environment, Paris, 4-6 October.

KNIBIEHLER, Y. (1994), "Combating Exclusion in Marseilles", paper presented to the OECD Conference on Women in the City: Housing, Services and the Urban Environment, Paris, 4-6 October.

LAUGHLIN, S. and Mc ILWAINE, G. (1994), "Women's Health Policy for Glasgow".

LITTLE, J. (1994), Gender, Planning and the Policy Process, Pergamon, Oxford.

LITTLE, J., PEAKE, L. and RICHARDSON, P. (1988), Women in Cities, Macmillan, Basingstoke.

MACFARLANE, L. (1993), "A Holistic Approach to Urban Problems, Strengthening Policy Action for and by Women", Urban Futures, Vol. 3, No. 3, December 1993.

MATHISEN, U. and SKJERVEN R., and Kari HUSABO, (1994) "A Woman"s Perspective in Public Planning – Municipal Planning on Women's Terms", paper presented to the OECD Conference on Women in the City: Housing, Services and the Urban Environment, Paris 4-6 October.

MATSUKAWA, J. (1994), "Tokyo Travel: Urban Space to Move Around Tokyo", paper presented to the OECD Conference on Women in the City: Housing, Services and the Urban Environment, Paris 4-6 October.

MICHEL, S. (1994), "Women and Planning – Not Love at First Sight", paper presented to the OECD Conference on Women in the City: Housing, Services and the Urban Environment, Paris, 4-6 October.

NIVARD, M. (1994), "Improving Education and Employment Opportunities for Women", paper presented to the OECD Conference on Women in the City: Housing, Services and the Urban Environment, Paris, 4-6 October.

MOSER, C. (1994), "Women, Gender and Urban Development Policy", paper presented to the OECD Conference on Women in the City: Housing, Services and the Urban Environment, Paris, 4-6 October.

NISANCIOGLU, S. (1994), "Participation of Women from the Community in the Urban Planning Process", paper presented to the OECD Conference on Women in the City: Housing, Services and the Urban Environment, Paris, 4-6 October.

NISANCIOGLU, S. (1994), "Accessing Retail Facilities: Open Sesame Project", paper presented to the OECD Conference on Women in the City: Housing, Services and the Urban Environment, Paris, 4-6 October.

Norway, Ministry of the Environment (1994) A Cookbook for Grassroots Planning.

Norway, Ministry of the Environment (1994) A Manual for Alternative Municipal Planning.

OECD (1994), Conference on Women in the City, National Report, Australia.

OECD (1994), Conference on Women in the City, National Report, Austria.

OECD (1994), Conference on Women in the City, National Report, Canada.

OECD (1994), Conference on Women in the City, National Report, Finland.

OECD (1994), Conference on Women in the City, National Report, Iceland.

OECD (1994), Conference on Women in the City, National Report, Germany.

OECD (1994), Conference on Women in the City, National Report, Portugal.

OECD (1994), Conference on Women in the City, National Report, Sweden.

OECD (1994), Conference on Women in the City, National Report, Turkey.

OECD (1994), Conference on Women in the City, National Report, United States.

OECD (1994), Report on Multi-Sectoral Approaches to Urban Regeneration.

SCHILEN, S. (1994), "Case Study: Grassroots Women Reclaiming and Rebuilding Community: Neighbourhood Women's Renaissance", paper presented to the OECD Conference on Women in the City: Housing, Services and the Urban Environment, Paris, 4-6 October.

THORBECK, S. (1991), "Gender in Two Slum Cultures, Environment and Urbanisation, Vol. 3, No. 2, October.

THORBECK, S. (1994), Gender and Slum Culture in Urban Asia, Zed Press, London.

TRUJILLO, C. H. (1994), "The Women in Human Settlements Development Programme", paper presented to the OECD Conference on Women in the City: Housing, Services and the Urban Environment, Paris, 4-6 October.

United Nations Centre for Human Settlements (Habitat) (1994), Women In Human Settlements Development Programme Discussion Paper for the UN Fourth World Conference on Women, Beijing, September 1994.

United Nations Centre for Human Settlements (Habitat) (1994), "Women's Participation in Habitat II: Introducing a Gender Perspective to the City Summit of 1996", special note to participants in OECD Conference on Women in the City, 4-6 October 1994.

Urban Futures (1993), Volume 3, Number 3, December; Special Issue with papers from Women and Planning Conference, Victoria, Australia, 8-9 July.

VON SCHWEINICHEN, C. (1994), "Presentation on Economic Commission for Europe", paper presented to the OECD Conference on Women in the City: Housing, Services and the Urban Environment, Paris, 4-6 October.

WEKERLE, G. (1994), "Violence Against Women: Safe Cities: Canadian Federal and Municipal Initiatives", paper presented to the OECD Conference on Women in the City: Housing, Services and the Urban Environment, Paris, 4-6 October.

WEKERLE, G. (1993), "Responding to Diversity: Housing Developed by and for Women", Canadian Journal of Urban Research, Volume 2, Number 2, December, pp. 95-113.

WILSON, E. (1994), "Cultural and Gender Concerns in Spatial Development", paper presented to the OECD Conference on Women in the City: Housing, Services and the Urban Environment, Paris, 4-6 October.

WILSON, E. (1991), The Sphinx in the City, Virago Press, London.

# ANNEXES

*Annex 1*


**Issue Paper: Women, gender and urban development policy,[1] by Dr Caroline Moser, World Bank**


*Introduction*

Do Third World urban women and the gendered aspects of urban development form a separate urban research agenda, or are such issues already adequately integrated into the existing research agendas? In reviewing the research agenda on women, gender and urban development over the past three decades, this paper examines the extent to which they have formed a separate agenda as against a part of mainstream research issues. In so doing it clarifies why urban gender issues have remained a marginal concern up to now, and identifies their critical importance for current agendas in the 1990s, in which "women's voices must enter the definition of development and the making of policy choices" (Sen and Grown, 1987).

The definition of any research agenda is a complex process. As the outset a useful distinction can be made between three research approaches to women in the developing world, that have critically influenced changing research agenda on urban women. First, gender-blind research is based on the assumption that "male is the norm". Such a "masculinist" mode of construction results in a failure to recognise the gendered construction of knowledge and the implications this has for defining research issues. Gender-blind research ignores, misunderstands or even trivializes such issues. Second, Women in Development (WID) research. The term "WID" was first coined in the early 1970s in the USA by a group of mainly female professionals and researchers, concerned with the increasing evidence that Third World development projects were negatively affecting women. It recognises that women are active participants in the development process, who through both their productive and reproductive roles provide a critical, if often unacknowledged contribution to economic growth. As an untapped resource, therefore, this approach argues that women must be "brought into" the development process.[2]

More recently recognition of the limitations of focusing on women in isolation has drawn attention to the need to look at Gender and Development (GAD), the third research approach. Underlying the fundamental shift from "women" to "gender" is the concern to look less at women's problems as perceived of in terms of their sex, in other words their biological differences with men, and more in terms of their gender, in other words the social relations between men and women, in which women have been systematically subordinated (Moser, 1993, p. 4).

Therefore WID tends to focus on women as a separate research category in its own right, to identify the issues important to women, and to provide solutions to assist them better participate in development processes by meeting practical gender needs. In contrast, the emphasis of GAD research is on the gender relations between men and women, and the specific manner in which these are temporally and spatially constructed-the way in which within such asymmetrical relations women are subordinated to men, with less access to, or control over resources. Solutions are less focused on women in isolation but on the means by which the balance in such asymmetrical relations might be shifted or changed, by meeting strategic gender needs (Moser, 1989, 1993).

Despite the conceptual distinctions between the WID and GAD research approaches, both share a number of common characteristics; such research is mainly done by women; their identification with other women and their common experiences often leads to a conflation of personal and professional arenas. Few men treat gender seriously in research, nor do many women. Indeed to be taken seriously at all as professionals many women ensure that they do not focus on women's issues.

In urban research this has been exacerbated by the fact that the realm of the "urban" as a planning domain has predominantly been defined in physical and spatial terms, linked to "men's" work, and dealing with such issues as transport, housing, land and infrastructure. These are associated with "hard" edged disciplines such as economics, planning, engineering, architecture, public administration and geography. In contrast, the "soft" social disciplines in which female researchers (but not issues of concern to women) predominate, such as sociology, demography and to a certain extent, anthropology, cover issues such as health, education and the family which are more commonly dealt with as separate national level sectoral concerns.

Finally, it is also important to distinguish between urban specific research, and research that includes women living in urban areas. While there is a body of work concerned to address the intersection of women/gender and the urban, there are far more studies which do so incidentally because the object of concern happens to be "located" in an urban place. This does not automatically transform them into issues OF the urban.

### The changing research agenda

Research on women, gender and urban development has not occurred in isolation. A clear relationship exists between macroeconomic development models and theoretical development paradigms, approaches to women and development, and urban research on women. Four distinct "periods" can be identified each dominated by a particular theoretical and policy development model. First, Modernisation and the Growth of Cities (1950-60s); second, Redistribution with Growth in Cities: Basic Needs (1970s – early 1980s); third, Management of Cities (early-mid 1980s); fourth, Response to Cities in Crisis (late 1980s-1990s).

A detailed review of research on women, gender and urban development during each of the four identified "periods" of Third World urban development highlights a number of important, clearly defined sequential stages – that get repeated in each of the four "periods" of urban development (if more transparently at later stages). Stage One is gender-blind research. Although more marked in the 1960s and 1970s than it is today, nevertheless gender-blindness still prevents many researchers from appreciating the pivotal nature of gender relations in determining women's participation in urban life, their roles in resolving urban problems and planning for urban futures.

Stage Two is "proving" that women are important, making them visible, in the urban development agenda addressed. Most of the work "counting women in" has been undertaken with a WID framework. This "add women and stir" research on "women and... housing, health, or water", etc., descriptively documents the participation of women in the different urban sector, but tends to focus on women as a separate category in themselves.

Stage Three shifts from women per se to gender. It is concerned with the identification of the manner and extent to which urban life is gendered, and the manner in which in different contexts the social construction of gender relations differentially constrain men and women's access to, and participation in, such areas of urban life. Undertaken within a GAD framework, this research is concerned with difference between women as well as between men and women.

Finally Stage Four is concerned with policy prescriptions and recommendations. Given the political difficulties and "cultural" sensitivities of prescriptions that address gender inequalities – strategic gender needs – most policy focused research shifts back to a WID framework, more comfortable addressing practical gender needs. However it is important to recognise that ultimately this will depend on who is defining policy, top-down policing policymakers or bottom-up stakeholder women. In each of the four identified "periods" of Third World urban development these four clearly differentiated stages occur. In the space available it is only possible to refer briefly to each period, highlighting as one particularly dramatic example, the case of informal sector research.

## Modernisation: women in male towns

In the first period, Modernisation and the Growth of Cities (1950s-1960s) most research was not "peopled" at all, but concerned with broad spatial and demographic trend measurements. An important exception was research on rural-urban migration and the problems of urban "integration" and "assimilation", undertaken mainly by anthropologists. Globally, rural gender divisions of labour determined the gendering of migration patterns. In African and Asian cities where such patterns were predominantly male, women were rarely included in the analysis, with references made either generally to "people" or specifically to men.

There is an ominous silence on women, for instance, in the early definitive work of anthropologists of the Manchester School of Urban Anthropology such as Max Gluckman (1958), Bill Epstein (1958), and Clyde Mitchell (1956) undertaken in urban sub-Saharan Africa. Thus in the debate about social change, Gluckman's famous comment "an African townsman is a townsman, an African miner is a miner" (1961, p. 69) referred specifically to men who migrated to the Copperbelt urban mining communities. Similarly, in his study of the "urbanisation" experience of Xhosa in East London, South Africa entitled Townsmen or Tribesmen, Philip Mayer referred throughout to the migrant as "he". Two separate chapters on "Girls and Women in Town" revealed a preoccupation with the way the sexual servicing such women provided contributed to the "immorality in towns" (Meyer, 1963, p. 252).[3]

Although Ester Boserup's seminal rural research had a critical impact on the development of WID policy, her urban work had far less policy impact, despite the fact that two thirds of her seminal book Women's Role in Economic Development focuses on urban areas, defined by Boserup as "Women in a Men's World". She identified "male towns' and semi-male towns'', where preference for male workers meant that women were increasingly being "left behind" in traditional rural activities. Her failure to recognise women's reproductive work allowing her to conclude, for instance, that in most Arab countries no more than some 5 per cent of women carry on any economic activity. "The remaining 95 per cent of adult women do little more than cooking the daily meals and taking care of children" (1970, p. 187).

## Women and the informal sector

By the late 1960s, "trickle down" failure, resulted in increasing preoccupation with poverty and unemployment. Redistribution with Growth: Basic Needs (1970s-early 1980s) emerged as the dominant development model. "Slum" and "shanty studies" identifying intra and inter-household reciprocal networks as critical mechanisms for survival, were, for the most, gender blind, or at best gender neutral. An interesting indicator of the focus on women is the number of references to "women" in the subject index.

For instance, in a number of "classic" Latin American slum studies of this period such as David Collier (1976) on Lima, Wayne Cornelius (1975) and Susan Eckstein (1977) on Mexico City, and Lisa Peattie (1970) on Ciudad Buayana, there are no references at all to women.

Predominant policy relevant research area during the 1970s focusing on the informal sector seriously underenumerated women. In 1981, Sethuraman, at the ILO, concluded in a nine city study in African, Asian and Latin American cities, "Female participation in the informal sector seems surprisingly low" (1981,190). ILO surveys were enterprise based, biased towards larger scale enterprises in the productive sector, and consequently "missed" the majority of women clustered in outwork, subcontracting and unrecognised work of wives in household enterprises. Equally they ignored the smaller one-person "enterprises" in the service and distributive sectors which in many contexts are predominated by women (Moser, 1984). Basic needs projects identified women in their reproductive role as beneficiaries of infrastructure such as water and sanitation. Although research on housing projects showed that "without the women the project would never have worked" (Chauhen, 19832,42), gender was not introduced as an analytical category, and the significant role that women played in community participation rarely mentioned in policy level research.[4]

By the 1970s, the influence of the second wave feminism of the late 1960s, and the establishment of the United Nation's Decade for Women, 1975-1985, resulted in a parallel research agenda. This was research on both WID and GAD, undertaken predominantly by women and seen as a separate areas of analysis.

It was to their role as producers that researchers turned, their objective, to "disprove" the ILO thesis that few women were in the informal sector. A proliferation of studies soon proved women were there, showing the critical importance of the informal sector as a source of income for women. Definitive studies such as Nirmala Banerjee (1981) on Calcutta; Mira Savara (1981) on Madras; Lourdes Arispe on Mexico City (1977); Marianne Schmink (1982) and Tom Merrick (1976) on Bela Horizone; Nici Nelson (1979) and Janet Bujra (1986) on Nairobi; Eleanor Wachtel (1975) on Nakuru; and Lee Jellinek (1978 on Jakarta documented and measured the high level of female informal sector participation.

Once women researchers had "proved" the presence of women in the informal sector, focus turned to the analysis of gender relations within the sector, shifting to a GAD framework. In Lima, MacEwen Scott for instance, concluded "the stereotyped image of employment in the informal sector is actually a more accurate description of women's jobs"[5] Petty commodity production research showed women's exploitation by the formal sector was not the only constraint confronted. With intense competition, gender was frequently used as an essential element in the divisions of labour, forcing women into less lucrative areas. (Moser, 1981, p. 28). Studies identified other gender related constraints in the informal sector such as unequal access to credit, because of lack of collateral, (Bruce, 1980; IWTC, 1985); lack of control over savings, highlighted in the important work of SEWA (the Self-Employed Women's Association) in Ahmedabad preventing enterprise expansion (Sebsted, 1982; Karl, 1983); lack of mobility due to child care responsibilities (Chant, 1987).

The policy implications of this research, however, were controversial. Questions about women's unpaid labour in household enterprises or their unequal access to credit could only be solved if women acquired greater control over resources and divisions of labour within the household were modified. Policy related research, therefore, tended to revert to a WID focus, addressing poor women as a separate category, developing measures to increase their income-generating options in gender-specific occupations, small in scale, to be developed by NGOs.[6]

### Women's urban struggle, infrastructure and housing needs

In the third period, The Management of Cities (1980s) the small pattern of different research approaches to women was repeated. Latin American research on this "crisis of collective consumption" and urban social movements mentioned women descriptively in passing. Castell's (1983) historical review, The City and the Grass Roots, recognised women's critical role in urban struggles but his analysis of their participation in terms of feminist consciousness failed to hypothesise the relationships between the women's movement and urban social movements. A very different complementary literature, concerned to reconstruct the same urban protest but from a feminist perspective, once again was designed to prove women were there – on the basis that "the actions and attitudes of men cannot be generalised to cover the entire population" (West and Blumburg, 1990,8). Important case studies were undertaken in Lima (Blondet, 1990; Andreas, 1985), Buenos Aires (Feijoo, 1990), and Guadalajara (Pardinas and Dieste, 1988).

Feminist researchers were concerned to document the role of women, not only as participants in struggle over items of collective consumption, but also, because of gendered divisions of labour, the manner in which they were managing the allocation, provisioning and maintenance of items of both household and community level consumption needs in cities (Moser, 1989a, 1993). Again, research went through a number of stages. WID focused research proved the importance of women's participation in community based service delivery (see Schmink, 1984, Schmink et al., 1986) – for instance, health issues in Sao Paulo (ISIS, 1985; Machado, 1991), childcare in Lima (Allyon Viana, 1982; Barrig and Fort, 1987) water in Guayaquil (Moser, 1987) and Tegucigalpa (Resources for Action, 1982); waste recycling in Mexico (Schmink, 1984, 1989); in collective construction in self-help housing in Guadalajara (Diaz, 1988), Panama (Girling, Lycette and Youssef, 1983) and Kingston, Jamaica (McLeod, 1989), Lusaka (Rakodi, 1983, Schlyter, 1988) and Nairobi (Nimpuno-Pariente, 1987); maintenance of community facilities in Colombo (Fernandez, 1987), village bus services in Kenya (Kneerim, 1989).

GAD focused research then identified the gendered nature of sectoral constraints, and the problems gender-blind urban planning imposed on women (see Moser, 1987a). These included transport routing in Brazil (Schmink, 1982); physical attacks in Peru (Anderson and Panzio, 1986). Research on the gendered nature of housing sector constraints included eligibility criteria in Brazil (Machado, 1987,62) and Quito (Lycette and Jaramillo, 1984); relocation affecting access to employment in Delhi (Sing, 1980); settlement design constraints in Lusaka (Schlyter, 1984); and zoning legislation in Nairobi (Nimpuno-Parente, 1987) to cite only a few.

Despite such search most policymakers at the time remained gender-blind. Thus, the United Nations Centre for Human Settlements (UNCHS) sponsored reassessment of critical shelter and human settlement problems edited by Lloyd Rodwin (1987) to coincide with the International Year of Shelter for the Homeless failed to contain a chapter on the particular gender needs of women, while all other chapters remained gender-blind.

During this period a number of important research areas developed which were not urban specific, but were predominantly identified as urban phenomena. These included the issue of household headship, and the limitations of planning stereotypes of nuclear families – with male breadwinners and women homemakers – resulting in research on urban households, particularly those headed by women. Secondly, the issue of intra-household resource allocation with great significance for policymakers concerned with targeted interventions for poverty alleviation. Third, by the 1980s, research on women's productive work prioritised formal sector labour market participation and the implications of changing global industrial processes for the restructuring for women's work – both the feminization, or "female-led industrialisation" of the industrial labour force in export zones, as well as the process of fractionalizing labour processes through sub-contracting and outwork, again to increase profits through lower factory costs and outwork wages. Here an important result was the introduction of gender disaggregated employment statistics.

*The urban consequences of "male bias" in structural adjustment policies*

Urban research since the mid 1980s, has been dominated by the global economic crisis and IMF and World Bank Macroeconomic reform packages of structural adjustment, designed to assist bankrupted economies onto the road of economic recovery. The most visible manifestations of this the fourth research period, Responses to Cities in Crises, has been state and local government inability to effectively manage and regulate urban life, accompanied by declines in the delivery, maintenance and quality of essential urban services such as water, electricity, transportation, health and education. Feminist research priorities have shifted from managing to coping with research focused at two levels.

First, research focused on the particular implications of male bias implicit in structural adjustment policies (SAPs), the gendered nature of such adjustment processes, and how women have been adversely affected. Male bias with specific urban implications include (Elson, 1991:6; Moser, 1992); first, the extent to which SAPs implicitly assumed that processes carried out by women in such unpaid activities as caring for children, gathering fuel, processing food, preparing meals, and nursing the sick, would continue regardless of the way in which resources are reallocated (Elson, 1991). With evidence still fragmentary, studies in Buenos Aires (Feijoo and Jelin, 1989) and Manila (Commonwealth Secretariat, 1989) questioned how far SAPs were successful at the cost of longer working days for women, forced to increase their labour both within the market and the household; preoccupation was expressed regarding the extent to which women's labour was infinitely elastic; (Jolly *et al.*, 1987); while empirical evidence from Guayaquil suggested changes in the balancing of time in women's triple role (Moser, 1992).

The second male "bias" concerned gender divisions of labour which ignored barriers to labour reallocation in policies designed to switch from non-tradeables to tradeables, offering incentives to encourage labour intensive manufacturing. In cities, this has meant unemployment for men displaced from non-tradeables, while for those women drawn into export oriented manufacturing, factory employment is added to domestic work which unemployed men remained reluctant to undertake, with examples from Brazil (Hirata and Humphrey, 1991). Evidence from Guadalajara (Gonzalez de la Rocha, 1988), Guayaquil (Moser, 1992), Queretaro (Chant, 1988; 1991, Chapter 6) and Mexico City (Beneria and Feldman, 1992) all showed increases in women's labour force participation, as well as changes in household composition – both a response to declining household income.

The third male bias concerned assumption of equal intra-household distribution of resources, which meant that changes in resource allocations in income, food prices and public expenditure, accompanying stabilisation and SAPs, affected all members of the household in the same way. Urban studies from Jamaica (Davies and Anderson, 1989), Mexico (Beneria, 1990) and Peru (Cornia *et al.*, 1987) showed that austerity measures altered the budgets of households, with poor families often eliminating meat, milk and other essential items from their diet. In Chile, women in poor households experienced more than commensurate declines in food intake during periods of declining food availability (Raczynski and Serrano, 1985). In Brazil, (Barroso and Amado, 1989) it has been alleged that the capacity of the household to shoulder the economic crisis has detrimentally affected human relationships, expressed in increased domestic violence and mental health disorder and increasing numbers of women-headed households resulting from the breakdown in nuclear family structures. In contrast, in Guadalajara the crisis forced men to surrender a larger portion of their wages to the household budget (de la Rocha, 1988).

Recognition of the limited potential to challenge "male bias" in SAPs resulted in a second policy focused research agenda, concerned to identify the constraints experienced by women due to lack of provision of basic services. Studies of low-income women's daily lives in cities such as Lima (Barrig and Fort, 1987), Quito (Rodriguez, 1990), Querétero (Chant, 1991), Sao Paulo

(Volbedas, 1989) and Oaxaca (Selby, 1991); Nairobi (Mitullah, 1991), Barnako (Vaale *et al.*, 1989) and urban Tanzania (Trip, 1989); and Madras (Noponen, 1991), all described the complex strategies women adopted to cope with the combined effect of declining income, increased food prices and a reduction in the level and composition of public expenditure on social sectors such as health education. Deriving out of this, alternative solutions for women have included community or communal kitchens (providing cheaper food while releasing women from domestic labour) in Lima (Sar-Lafosse, 1984), and women's food plots (to improve household nutrition) in Lusaka (Rakodi, 1988), peri-urban Gambia (Barrett and Browne, 1988) and Nairobi (Freeman, 1991).

## *Conclusion: Cities and sustainable development: challenges for the 1990s*

The review of research agendas highlights three important issues with significant implications for future research. First, over the past three decades there has been a remarkable body of both WID and GAD urban research. However, most of it has had little influence on mainstream urban researchers or on policymakers. Other than some of recent research on employment and urban labour markets, mainstream urban development research remains essentially gender-blind.

Second, most of this research is still a specialist concern, undertaken by women in separate departments or work areas. This has effectively marginalized much of their work, as well as affecting the career choices of both women and men researchers. Third, when such research has been taken seriously by policymakers, they have generally felt more comfortable with WID focused research, choosing to address interventions that assist women within their existing roles in society, rather than those that challenge gender divisions of labour or the nature of gender subordination. Therefore, as long as research on women remains an "add on", the results remain outside of mainstream urban policy and fail to influence important policy agendas.

For many researchers the first priority for the 1990s is the mainstreaming of what is still a separate specialist concern, and its translation into policy and practice. One of the most important options is to clarify why this body of research remains unintegrated. Are the constraints technical or political in nature? (Moser, 1993, Chapter 1). Is the problem that "policy" is essentially "policing" and that in their recommendations the purpose of policymakers is to control rather than empower local women. Researchers need to address these types of questions if they are to identify the entry points to effectively operationalize and institutionalise their results into mainstream urban research and policy.

Obviously, there are also a number of continuing, as well as new, research agendas for the 1990s requiring a paper in itself, with space here for only a final non-inclusive checklist. This includes:

- listening to women and hearing what they say;
- differences between women in the urban context;
- finding a meeting point between approaches that emphasise commonalties as against differences between women;
- new methodologies for gendered research that allow women themselves to identify their similarities and differences;
- women, citizenship, democratisation and decentralisation, to date the role of women in local municipal government one of the few areas addressed;
- women, social unrest and violence, a continuum that begins within the household and reaches beyond as it becomes a community and city-wide problem;
- gender and the urban environment, still without a comprehensive analytical framework to identify how the urban environment is gendered.

# Notes

1. This article is an abridged and amended synthesis of some of the main issues in C. Moser (with L. Peake) "Seeing the Invisible: Women, Gender and Urban Development" in R. Stren (ed.) Urban Research in the Developing World: Volume 4 Thematic Issues, Toronto: Centre for Urban and community Studies, University of Toronto (forthcoming). This extensive review article was undertaken as an advisory panel member to the Ford Foundation funded research project on Urban Research in the Developing World. I would like to acknowledge the important contribution of Richard Stren and Judith Kjelberg Bell, of the Toronto research project.

2. For a detailed discussion of the historical development of WID and GAD and the important distinctions between them see Moser (1993, Chapter 1).

3. Mayer was assisted in this study by his wife, Iona Mayer.

4. Moser (1989) reviews community participation in urban projects, evaluating self-help housing projects undertaken by multilaterals, national governments and NGOs, from a gender perspective.

5. See A.M. Scott (1989) for a later more developed description of the thesis.

6. Buvinic (1986) has highlighted the problems experienced by anti-poverty projects in the implementation process.

# References

ANDERSON, J. and PANZIO, N. (1986), "Transportation and public safety: Services that make service use possible" in Schmink, M., Bruce, J. and Kohn, M. (eds.) (1986). Learning about Women and Urban Services in Latin America and the Caribbean. New York: The Population Council.

ANDREAS, C. (1985), When Women Rebel: The rise of popular feminism in Peru. Connecticut: Lawrence Hill.

ARIZPE, L. (1977), "Women in the Informal Labor Sector: The Case of Mexico City". Signs 3, No. 1, pp. 25-37.

AYLLON VIANA, R. (1982), "Organizacion de una guaderia infantil con la poblacion femenina del Pueblo Joven Huascar". Paper presented at the research conference on Women in the Andean Region. Lima.

BANERJEE, J. (1981), "The Weakest Link". Institute of Development Studies Bulletin, 12,3.

BARRETT, H. and BROWNE, A. (1988), "Women's horticulture in the peri-urban zone, the Gambia". Geography 73, No. 2, pp. 158-160.

BARRIG, M. and FORT, A. (1987), "La Ciudad de las Mujeres: Pobladoras y Servicios, El Caso de El Augustino". Women, Low-Income Households and Urban Services Working Papers, Lima.

BARROSO, C. and AMADO, T. (1989), "Impact of this crisis on the health of poor urban women; The case of Brazil" in UNICEF (ed.). The Invisible Adjustment: Poor Women and the Economic Crisis. Bogota: UNICEF.

BENERIA, L. and FELDMAND, D. (eds.) (1992), Unequal Burden: Economic Crises, Persistent Poverty and Women's Work, Boulder, Westview Press.

BLONDET, C. (1990), "Establishing an identity: Women settlers in a poor Lima neighbourhood" in Jelin, E. (ed.). Women and Social Change in Latin America. London: Zed.

BOSERUP, E. (1970), Woman's Role in Economic Development. New York: St. Martins Press.

BRUCE, J. (1980), Market Women's Co-operatives: Giving Women Credit. New York: Population Council.

BUJRA, J. (1986), "Urging women to redouble their efforts... Class gender and capitalist transformation in Africa" in C. Robertson and I. Berger (eds.). Women and Class in Africa, pp. 117-40. New York: Africana Publishing Company.

CASTELLS, M. (1983), The City and the Grassroots. London: Edward Arnold.

CHANT, S. (1987), "Family Structure and Female Labour in Queretero, Mexico" in J. Momsen and J. Townsend (eds.). Geography of Gender in the Third World. London: Hutchinson.

CHANT, S. (1991), Women and Survival in Mexican Cities: Perspectives on Gender, Labour Markets, and Low-Income Households. Manchester: St. Martin's Press.

CHANT, S. and BRYDEN, L. (1989), Women in the Third World. Aldershot: Edward Elgar.

CHAUHEN, S. (ed.) (1983), "Green Flag Over Baldia Pit Latrines", in Who Puts The Water In The Taps? London: Earthscan.

COLLIER, D. (1976), Squatters and Oligarchs: Authoritarian Rule and Policy Change in Peru. Baltimore: John Hopkins University Press.

Commonwealth Secretariat (1989), Engendering Adjustment for the 1990s: Report of the Commonwealth Expert Group on Women and Structural Adjustment. London: Commonwealth Secretariat.

CORNELIUS, W. (1975), Politics and the Migrant Poor in Mexico City. Stanford: Stanford University Press.

CORNIA, G., JOLLY, R., and STEWART, F. (eds.) (1987), Adjustment with a Human Face, Vol. 1. Oxford: Oxford University Press.

DAIZ, L. (1988), "El papel de la mujer en la autoconstruccion de vivienda, Zona Metropolitana de Guadelajara" in Gabayet et al. (eds.). Mujeres y Sociedad: Salario, Hogar y Accion social en el Occidente de México, Guadalajara, el Colegio de Jalisco.

DAVIES, O. and ANDERSON, A. (1989), "The impact of the recession and adjustment policies on poor urban women in Jamaica" in UNICEF (ed.). The Invisible Adjustment: Poor Women and the Economic Crisis. Bogota: UNICEF.

ECKSTEIN, S. (1977), The Poverty of Revolution: The State and the Urban Poor in Mexico. Princeton: Princeton University Press.

ELSON, D. (1991), "Male Bias in Macroeconomics: The Case of Structural Adjustment" in Elson, D. (ed.). Male Bias in the Development Process. Manchester: Manchester University Press.

FEIJOO, J. del C. and GOGNA, J. (1990), "Women in the Transition to Democracy" in Jelin, E. (ed.). Women and Social Change in Latin America, London: Zed.

FEIJOO, M. del C. and JELIN, E. (1989), "Women from low income sectors: Economic recession and democratization of politics" in UNICEF (ed.). The Invisible Adjustment: Poor Women and the Economic Crisis. Bogota: UNICEF.

FERNANDO, M. (1987), "New Skills for Women: A Community Development Project in Colombo, Sri Lanka" in Moser, C.O.N. and Peake, L. (eds.). Women, Human Settlements and Housing. London: Tavistock.

FREEMAN, D. (1991), A City of Farmers: Informal Urban Agriculture in the Open Spaces of Nairobi, Kenya. Kingston: McGill-Queens University Press.

GIRLING, R., LYCETTE, M. and YOUSSEF, N. (1983), A Preliminary Examination of the Panama Self-Help Women's Construction Project. Washington, D.C.: International Centre for Research on Women.

GONZALEZ DE LA ROCHA, M. (1988), "Economic crisis, domestic reorganization and women's work in Guadalajara, Mexico" in Bulletin of Latin American Research, 7,2, pp. 207-223.

HIRATA, H. and HUMPHREY, J. (1991), "Worker's Response to Job Loss: Female and Male Industrial Workers in Brazil" World Development 19, No. 6, pp. 671-682.

IWTC (International Women's Tribune Centre) (1985), "Women, Money and Credit", Newsletter 15. New York: IWTC.

146

ISIS (1985), "Women and health: The Brazilian experience", ISIS International Women's Journal, No. 3.

JELLENICK, L. (1978), "Circular migration and the pondok dwelling system: A case study of ice-cream traders in Jakarta', in P. Rimmer, D. Drakakis-Smith and T.G. McGee (eds.). Food, Shelter and Transport in Southeast Asia and the Pacific, Canberra: Australian National University.

JOLLY, R., "Women's Needs and Adjustment policies in Developing Countries", an address to the Women's Development Group of the OECD, Paris.

KARL, M. (1983), "Women and Rural Development", in Women in Development: A Resource Guide. Geneva: ISIS Collective.

KNEERIM, J. (1989), "Village women organize: The Mararu Kenya Bus Service", in Leonard, A. (ed.). Seeds: Supporting Women's Work in the Third World. New York: Feminist Press.

LYCETTE, M. and JARAMILLO, C. (1984), Low-Income Housing: A Woman's Perspective. Washington, D.C.: International Center for Research on Women.

MACHADO, L. (1987), "The problems for women-headed households in a low-income housing programme in Brazil", in Moser, C. and Peake, L. (eds.). Women, Human Settlements and Housing. London: Tavistock.

MAYER, P. (1963), Townsmen or Tribesmen. Cape Town: Oxford University Press.

MCLEOD, R. (1989), "The Kingston Women's Construction Collective: Building for the future in Jamaica" in Leonard, A. (ed.). Seeds: Supporting Women's Work in the Third World. New York: Feminist Press.

MERRICK, T. (1976), "Employment and earnings in the informal sector in Brazil: The case of Belo Horizonte", Journal of Developing Areas 10,3.

MITULLAH, W. (1991), "Hawking as a survival strategy for the urban poor in Nairobi: The case of women". Environment and Urbanization 3, No. 2, pp. 13-22.

MOSER, C.O.N. (1993), Gender Planning and Development: Theory, Practice and Training. London: Routledge.

MOSER, C.O.N. (1992), "Adjustment From Below: Low-Income Women, Time and the Triple Role in Guayaquil, Ecuador" in Afshar, H. and Dennis, C. (eds.). Women and Adjustment Policies in the Third World. Basingstoke: Macmillan.

MOSER, C.O.N. (1989a), "Gender Planning in the Third World: Meeting practical and Strategic Gender Needs", Word Development, Vol. 17, No. 11.

MOSER, C.O.N. (1989b), "Community Participation in Urban Projects in the Third World". Progress in Planning, Vol. 32, Part 2.

MOSER, C.O.N. (1987b), "Mobilization in Women's Work: Struggles for Infrastructure in Guayaquil, Ecuador", in Moser, C.O.N. and Peake, L. (eds.). Women, Human Settlements and Housing. London: Tavistock.

MOSER, C.O.N. (1984), "The Informal Sector Reworked: Viability and Vulnerability in Urban Development", Regional Development Dialogue, Vol. 5, No. 2.

MOSER, C.O.N. (1981), "Surviving in the Suburbios", Institute of Development Studies Bulletin, Vol. 12, No. 3.

NELSON, N. (1979), "How women and men get by: The sexual division of labour in the informal sector of a Nairobi squatter settlement", in Bromley, R. and Gerry, C. (eds.). Casual Work and Poverty in Third World Cities. London: Wiley.

NIMPUNO-PARENTE, P. (1987), "The Struggle for Shelter: Women in a Site and Service Project in Nairobi, Kenya", in Moser, C.O.N. and Peake, L. (eds.). Women, Human Settlements and Housing. London: Tavistock.

NOPONEN, H. (1991), "The dynamics of work and survival for the urban poor: A gender analysis of panel data from Madras". Development and Change 22, No. 2, pp. 233-260.

PARDINAS, D.L. and DIESTE, C.P. in Gabayet et al. (eds.) (1988), Mujeres y Sociedad: Salario, Hogar y Accion social en el Occideiente de México. Guadalajara: el Colegio de Jalisco.

PEATTIE, L. (1968), The View from the Barrio. Ann Arbor: University of Michigan Press.

RACZYNSKI, D. and SERRANO, C. (1985), Vivir al Pobresa. Testimonios de Mujeres. Santiago: CIEPLANPISPAL.

RAKODI, C. (1988), "Urban agriculture: Research questions and Zambian evidence". Journal of Modern African Studies 26, No. 3, pp. 495-515.

RAKODI, C. (1983), "The World Bank Experience: Mass community Participation in the Lusaka Squatter Upgrading Project", in Moser, C. (ed.). Evaluating Community Participation in Urban Development Projects, Development Planning Unit Working Paper No. 14. London.

Resources for Action (1982a), Women and Shelter in Tunisia: A Survey of the Shelter Needs of Women in Low-Income Areas. Washington, D.C.: USAID Office of Housing.

RODWIN, Lloyd (1987), Lloyd SHELTER, Settlement and Development, London.

RODRIQUEZ, L. (1990), Las Mujeres de Solanda, Quito, CEPAM-ILDES.

SARA-LAFOSSA, V. (1984), Comedores Comunales: La Mujer Frente A La Crisis, (Lima: Grupo de Trabajo). Lima: Servicios Urbanos y Mujeres de Bajos Ingresos.

SAVALA, M. (1981), "Organizing the Annapurna", Institute of Development Studies Bulletin, 12, July.

SCHMINK, M. (1989), "Community Management of Waste Recycling in Mexico: The SIRDO" in Leonard, A. (ed.). Seeds: Supporting Women's Work in the Third World. New York: The Feminist Press.

SCHMINK, M. (1984), "the Working Group Approach to Women and Urban Services" (mimeo). Gainsville: Centre for Latin American Studies, University of Florida.

SCHMINK, M. (1984), Community Management of Waste Recycling; The Sirdo. New York: Population Council.

SCHMINK, M. (1982), "Women in the Urban Economy in Latin America", Population Council Working Paper No. 1. New York: The Population Council.

SCHMINK, M., BRUCE, J. and KOHN, M. (eds.) (1986), Learning about Women and urban Services in Latin America and the Caribbean. New York: The Population Council.

SCHLYTER, A. (1988), Women Householders and Housing Strategies: The Case of George. Lund: The National Swedish Institute for Building Research.

SELBY, H. (1991), "The Oaxacan urban household and the crisis". Urban Anthropology 20, No. 1, pp. 87-98.

SEN, G. and L. GROWN, (1987), Development, Crises, and Alternative Visions: Third World perspectives. New York: Monthly Review Press.

SETHURAMAN, S.V. (ed.) (1981), The Urban Informal Sector in Developing Countries: Employment, Poverty and Environment. (A WEP Study) Geneva: ILO.

SINGH, A. (1980), Women in Cities: an Invisible Factor in urban Planning in India (mimeo). New York: Population Council.

148

TRIPP, A. (1989), "Women and the changing urban household economy in Tanzania". Journal of Modern African Studies 27, No. 4, pp. 601-623.

VAAL, M., S. FINDLEY and A. DIALLO. (1989), "The gift economy: A study of women migrants survival strategies in a low-income Bambako neighbourhood". Labour, Capital and Society 22, No. 2, pp. 234-260.

VOLBEDA, S. (1989), "Housing and survival strategies of women in metropolitan slum areas in Brazil". Habitat International 13, No. 3, pp. 157-171.

WACHTEL, E. (1975), "Minding Her Own Business: Economic Enterprises of Women in Nakuru, Kenya". Canadian Association of African Studies, 5th Annual Conference, 19-22 February. Toronto: Ontario.

WEST, G. and BLUBMERG, R. (eds.), Women and Social Protest. New York: Oxford University Press.

*Annex 2*

# LIST OF PARTICIPANTS

**OECD Conference on Women in the City:
Housing, Services and the Urban Environment Paris, 4-6 October 1994**

**OECD Member countries**

## AUSTRALIA – AUSTRALIE

HEAD OF DELEGATION

Ms. Lynne Gallagher
Special Advisor
Department of Housing and Regional
Development
G.P.O. Box 9834
Canberra
ACT 2601

OFFICIAL DELEGATION

Ms. Sallyanne Atkinson AO
Senior Trade Commissioner
AUSTRADE
4, rue Jean-Rey
75724 Paris
FRANCE

Dr. Renate Howe (Chair of Session on
Housing and the Neighbourhood
Environment)
Associate Professor
Faculty of Arts
Deakin University
VIC 3217

Ms. Patricia Kelly
Acting First Secretary
Office of the Status of Women
Department of the Prime Minister and
Cabinet
3-5 National Circuit
Barton
ACT 2600

Ms. Andrea Thrift
Better Cities Section
Department of Housing and Regional
Development
G.P.O. Box 9834
Canberra
ACT 2601

OTHER PARTICPANTS

Ms. Caroline Denigan
Women's Self Built Housing
Support Network
16 Warnvale Drive
Belmont
VIC 3216

Ms. Sylvia Der
Architect
Department of Planning and Development
44 Murray Street
West Brunswick
VIC 3055

Ms. Trish Ferrier
392 Swan Road
St. Lucia
QLD 4067

Ms. Kylie Fox
Lecturer
School of Building and Planning
University of South Australia
North Terrace
Adelaide
SA 5000

Ms. Louise Glanville
Senior Lecturer
Department of Urban and Social Policy
Faculty of Arts
Victoria University of Technology
P.O. Box 14428
Melbourne Mail Centre
Melbourne
VIC 3001

Ms. Leisha Host
Social Worker
SQWISI
P.O. Box 5689
Westend
QLD. 4101

Ms. Margo Huxley
Associate Professor
Department of Planning, Policy and
Landscape
Faculty of Environmental Design and
Construction
Royal Melbourne Institute of Technology
GPO Box 2476V
Melbourne
VIC 3001

Ms. Angela Jurjevic
Director of Housing Services
Department of Planning and Development
17th. Floor Myer House
250 Elizabeth Street
Melbourne
VIC 3000

Mr. James A. "Chip" Kaufman
Principal and Urban Designer
Ecologically Sustainable Design
243 Kean Street
North Fitzroy
VIC 3068

Ms. Diana Leeder
Community Services Manager
Darwin City Council
Civic Centre
GPO Box 84
Darwin
NT 0801

Ms. Wendy Morris
Deputy Manager
Urban Design Unit
Department of Planning and Development
GPO Box 2240T
Melbourne
VIC 3001

Ms. Nyambura Mwaniki
Urban and Regional Planner/Researcher
University of Sydney
49/19-25 Queen Street
Newtown
NSW 2042

Ms. Carolyn Ozturk
Director
COMMARC Australia
149 Parry Street
Perth
WA 6000

Ms. Susan Parham
South Australian Department of
Housing and Urban Development
GPO Box 667
Adelaide
SA 5000

Ms. Denise Payne
15 Currajong Road
East Hawthorn
VIC 3123

Mr. Robert Solly
Director of Housing
Department of Planning and Development
17th Floor
250 Elizabeth Street
Melbourne
VIC 3000

Ms. Mary-Lynne Taylor
Taylor-Szekeouk-Kelso
Level 7, 16 O'Connell Street
Sydney
NSW 2000

# AUSTRIA – AUTRICHE

HEAD OF DELEGATION

Ms. Eva Kail (Presenter)
Head
Administration of the City of Vienna
Municipal Department: Promotion and
Co-ordination of Women's Affairs
Friedrich-Schmidt-Platz 3
A-1082 Vienna

OFFICIAL DELEGATION

Ms. Ursula Bauer (Presenter)
City Planner
Administration of the City of Vienna
Municipal Department: Promotion and
Co-ordination of Women's Affairs
Friedrich-Schmidt-Platz 3
A-1082 Vienna

# BELGIUM – BELGIQUE

HEAD OF DELEGATION

Mr. Fons Famaey
Director
Department of Social Affairs,
Public Health and Environment
City of Antwerp
van Immerseel straat 11
2018 Antwerp

OTHER PARTICIPANTS

Mme Françoise Galloudec
Institut international des sciences
administratives
Conseiller scientifique
1, rue Defacqz
B-1040 Bruxelles

Mme Rottiers
Valkerygang 26
3000 Louvain

PERMANENT DELEGATION
TO THE OECD

M. Roger Brulard
Conseiller à la représentation permanente

# CANADA

## HEAD OF DELEGATION

Ms. Karen Kinsley
Vice-President, Finance,
Canadian Mortgage and Housing
Corporation
National Office
700 Montreal Road
Ottawa
Ontario K1A OP7

## OFFICIAL DELEGATION

Ms. Jean Augustine MP
(Chair of the Conference)
Vice-Chair
Ministerial Task Force on Social Policy
Reforms
Member of the Parliamentary Committee on
Human Resource Development
Parliamentary Secretary to the Prime
Minister
Room 125
Confederation Building
House of Commons
Ottawa
Ontario K1A OA6

Ms. Charlotte Clouthier
Director of Policy Analysis and
Development
Status of Women-Canada
Ottawa

Ms. Cassi Doyle
Deputy Minister
Housing, Recreation and Consumer Services
Province of British Columbia
6th Floor
1019 Wharf Street
Victoria
BC V8V 1X4

Ms. Sylvia Haines
Executive Assistant to the
Parliamentary Secretary to the Prime
Minister
Confederation Building
House of Commons
Ottawa
Ontario K1A OA6

Ms. Janet Kiff-Macaluso (Rapporteur/
Presenter)
Manager
Social Policy Division
Canadian Mortgage and Housing
Corporation
National Office
700 Montreal Road
Ottawa
Ontario K1A OP7

Ms. Anne Michaud
Manager
Women and the City
City of Montreal

Mr. Peter Paproski
Senior Adviser
Urban Development Branch
Canadian International Development Agency
200 Promenade du Portage, 11th. Floor
Hull
Quebec K1A OG4

Mr. Peter Spurr
Senior Officer
International Relations Division
Canadian Mortgage and Housing Corpora-
tion
National Office
700 Montreal Road
Ottawa
Ontario K1A OP7

Professor Gerda Wekerle (Presenter)
Faculty of Environmental Studies
York University
4700 Keele Street
North York
Ontario M3J 1P3

# FINLAND – FINLANDE

## HEAD OF DELEGATION

Ms. Sirpa Pietikäinen (Chair of Session on
Urban Services Responsive to
Diverse Needs)
Minister of the Environment
Ministry of the Environment
Ratakatu 3
P.O. Box 399
SF-00121 Helsinki

## OFFICIAL DELEGATION

Ms. Sirkka Hautojärvi
Acting Secretary General
Ministry of the Environment
Ratakatu 3
P.O. Box 399
SF-00121 Helsinki

Mr. Seppo Heinänen
Deputy Mayor
City of Vantaa
Kaupungintalo
Asematie 7
PL 5
SF-01301 Vantaa

Ms. Sirpa Hertell-Westerlund
Secretary General
Member of City Board of Espoo
Eerikinkatu 24 A 7
SF-00100 Helsinki

Dr. Liisa Horelli (Presenter)
Consulting Researcher
Technical University of Helsinki
Architectural Department
Hopeasulmentie 21 B
SF-00570 Helsinki

Ms. Ulla-Maija Laiho
Special Adviser
The Association of Finnish Local Authorities
Suomen Kuntaliitto
2 linja 14
SF-00530 Helsinki

Ms. Elina Lehto
Mayor
City of Hämeenlinna
Kaupungintalo
PL 87
SF-13101 Hämeenlinna

Mr. Jukka Noponen
Head of Department
Soil and Water Ltd.
Centre for Urban and Regional Studies
Helsinki University of Technology
Maa ja Vesi Oy
Itälahdenkatu 2
SF-00210 Helsinki

Ms. Aija Staffans
Architect
Helsinki University of Technology
Urban Design and Planning
Department of Architecture
Otakaari 1 X
SF-02150 Espoo

Ms. Eeva-Liisa Tuominen
Secretary General
Office of Equality Ombudsman
PL 267
SF-00171 Helsinki

## OTHER PARTICIPANTS

Ms. Riita Haverinen
Erikoissuunnittelija
STAKES
Siltasaarenkatu 18, Pl. 220
00531 Helsinki

Dr. Pirio Carita Immonen-Räihä
Senior Researcher
Health Office of the City of Turku
Turun terveydenhuolto, Sakke
Pl 11
20701 Turku

Ms. Kari Mattila
Counsellor
Unionen r.f.
Östra Strandr 7
92230 Esbo

# FRANCE

## HEAD OF DELEGATION

M. Georges Cavallier (Vice-Chairman-Group
on Urban Affairs/Rapporteur)
Ingénieur général des
ponts et chaussées
38, rue Liancourt
F-75014 Paris

## OFFICIAL DELEGATION

Mme Françoise de Veyrinas
Député européen
Maire adjoint de Toulouse
Toulouse

Mme Marguerite Arène
Chargée de mission à la Délegation
interministerielle à la ville
194, avenue, Président Wilson
93217 La Plaine-St.-Denis Cedex

Mme Michèle Brielle
Chargée de mission
Conseil général des ponts et chaussées
Ministère de l'Équipement, des Transports
et du Tourisme
Paris

M. Vincent Delbos
Chargé de mission responsable
des affaires internationales
Délégation interministérielle à la ville
Paris

Mme Evelyne Hardy
Chargée de mission
Ministère de l'Équipement, des Transports
et du Tourisme
Paris

M. Hervé Huntzinger
Consultant
Bureau d'études TETRA
20, rue Malher
Paris 75004

Mme Monique Minaca (Presenter)
Architecte conseil, économiste-urbaniste
Groupe cadre de vie
60, avenue Jean-Jaurès
92190 Meudon

Mme Françoise Reynaud
Institut des sciences et techniques
de l'équipement et de l'environnement
pour le développement (ISTEED)
Paris

## OTHER PARTICIPANTS

Mme Suzanne Alexandre
290, avenue de Fabron
06200 Nice

Mme Brigitte Babin
Directrice adjointe
CNIDFF
7, rue du Jura
75017 Paris

Mme Dowelle Barichasse
Chargée de mission
Service des droits des femmes
Ministère des Affaires sociales,
de la Santé de la ville
31, rue Pelletier
75009 Paris

Dr. Rabia Bekkar
Enseignante/Chercheur
IPRAUS
Université de Paris-X Nanterre
116, rue d'Alésia
75014 Paris

Mme Jane Bisillat
ORSTOM
213, rue Lafayette
75010 Paris

Mme Martine Boiteux
Ministère de l'Enseignement supérieure
et de la Recherche
Délégation aux relations européennes
et francophones
1, rue Descartes
75005 Paris

Mme Sandra Ceciarini
Responsable Information
Conseil des communes et régions d'Europe
41, quai d'Orsay
75007 Paris

Mme Anne Cogne
Élue municipale
Mairie de Rennes
35000 Rennes

M. Christian Cucchiarini (Presenter)
Syndicat national de l'entreprise générale
SNBATI
9, rue La Pérouse
75784 Paris
Cedex 16

Mme Chantal Duchène (Presenter)
Chef de départment
Centre d'études des transports urbains
(CETUR)
8, avenue Aristide-Briand
32220 Bagneux

Mme Hinokidani
Centre de sociologie urbaine (CNRS)
Paris

M. Jean-Marie Joly
Directeur du bâtiment
et directeur du développement
SOGEA
3, cours Ferdinand-de-Lesseps
92851 Rueil-Malmaison Cedex

Mme Yvonne Knibiehler (Presenter)
Président
Association "Les femmes et la ville"
7, parc Mozart
13100 Aix-en-Provence

Mme Mireille de Laval
Adjointe au maire déléguée aux personnes
agées au CCAS, à la famille et à la
solidarité
Ville de Marseille
11, boulevard des Dames
13002 Marseille

Mme Marie-Francoise Legrand
Directrice de la mission de
développement social et urbain
UNFOHLM
14, rue Lord-Byron
75008 Paris

Mme Eleanor Levieux
148, rue de Lourmel
75015 Paris

M. Michel Marcus
Délégué général
Forum européen pour la sécurité urbaine
38, rue Liancourt
75014 Paris

Mme Isabelle Marguerite
ADRI
4, rue René-Villermée
75011 Paris

Mme Noëlle Marillier
Chef du bureau droits propres
Service des droits des femmes
Ministère des Affaires sociales,
de la Santé de la ville
31, rue Pelletier
75009 Paris

Mme Martine Nivard (Presenter)
Déléguée générale
Association Retravailler
21, passage Gustave Lepeu
Paris 75011

Mme Anne Querrien
Rédacteur en chef des annales
de la recherche urbaine
Plan urbain
METT-Tour Pascal B.
92055 Paris La Defense

Mme Michèle Ramadier
Conseiller municipal déleguée aux
crèches et aux droits des femmes
Association des crèches
Atrium Bt. B.
4, avenue Marcel-Pagnol
13090 Aix-en-Provence

Mme Sophie Régnauld
Attaché principal
Direction générale culture, education
et sport
Ville de Rennes
BP 3126
35031 Rennes
Cedex

Mme Béatrice Romet
ATCCRE
30, rue d'Alsace-Lorraine
45100 Orléans

Mlle Sophie Rousseau
Consultante
Observatoire européen du logement social
et de ''Euro-Conception'' (via le
CRESSAC)
44, avenue du Général-de-Gaulle
94160 Saint-Mandé

M. Louis Servant
Expert Transport
METROPOLIS
251, rue de Vaugirard
75015 Paris

Mme Zago-Koch
Service des droits des femmes
Ministère des Affaires sociales,
de la Santé de la ville
31, rue Pelletier
75009 Paris

# GERMANY – ALLEMAGNE

## HEAD OF DELEGATION

Ms. Susanne Messing (Member-Group on
Urban Affairs)
Federal Ministry for Regional Planning,
Building and Urban Development
Bundesministerium für Raumordnung
Bauwesen und Städtebau
Deichmanns Aue 31-37
53179 Bonn

## OFFICIAL DELEGATION

Dr. Brigitte Adam
Bundesforschungsanstalt für
Landeskunde und Raumordnung
Am Michaelshof 8
53177 Bonn

Ms. Gabriele Kotzke
Stadtplanung - Moderation -
Planungsberatung
Stellinger Weg 8
20255 Hamburg

## OTHER PARTICIPANTS

Dr. Kerstin Doerhoefer
Professor
Hochschule der Künste, Berlin
Postfach 126720
D-10595 Berlin

Ms. Marita Estor (Presenter)
President
OECD Working Party on the Role
of Women in the Economy
In der Gemoll 33
35037 Marurg an der Lahn

Ms. M. Kampmann
WID/SAD Coordinator
GTZ
P.O. Box 5180
65726 Eschborn

Dr. Marianne Rodenstein
Professor
Universität Frankfurt
WBE Produktion/Sozialstruktur
Robert-Mayerstr. 5
60054 Frankfurt/Main

Ms. Meike Spitzner
Senior Scientist
Transport Division
Wuppertal-Institute for Climate,
Environment and Energy
Doppersberg 19
D-42103 Wuppertal

Dr. Ulla Terlinden
Professor in Fuer Stadt Soziologie
Technische Universitaet
Berlin Fachbereich 7
Doves Prase 1
D-10587 Berlin

# GREECE – GRÈCE

## HEAD OF DELEGATION

Mr. Agelos Agelidis
Architect
Manpower Employment Organisation
(OAED)
88 Thrakis Street
Trahones
16610 Athens

## OFFICIAL DELEGATION

Ms. Avra Kiriopoulou
Architect
Organisation for Planning and
Environmental Protection of Athens
2 Panormou Street
11523 Athens

Ms. Eugenia Melabianaki
Architect
Public Spaces Design
Architectural Design
Municipality of Athens
22 Liossion Street
10438 Athens

## OTHER PARTICIPANTS

Ms. Ekaterini Daskalaki
Municipal Councellor
Municipality of Athens
Ksenias 1
14562 Kifisia

Dr. Dina Vaiou
Assistant Professor of Planning
Department of Urban and Regional Planning
N. Technical University of Athens
Pylarinou 10 - Papagiou
15669 Athens

# ICELAND – ISLANDE

## HEAD OF DELEGATION

Ms. Ingibjörg Solrun Gisladottir
Mayor of Reykjavik
Borgarskrifstofur
Radhus Reykjavik
101 Reykjavik

## OFFICIAL DELEGATION

Ms. Kristin Arnadottir
Assistant to the Mayor of Reykjavik
Borgarskrifstofur
Radhus Reykjavik
101 Reykjavik

# IRELAND – IRLANDE

## HEAD OF DELEGATION
## OFFICIAL DELEGATION
## OTHER PARTICIPANTS

Ms. Helen Blake
Apt. 40 Ha'penny Bridge House
Lower Ormond Quay
Dublin 1

# ITALY – ITALIE

HEAD OF DELEGATION

OFFICIAL DELEGATION

OTHER PARTICIPANTS

Professor Carmen Belloni (Presenter)
Department of Social Sciences
University of Turin
10124 Torino Via S. Ottavio, 50
Professeur Paola Somma
Dipartimento DAEST Istituto
Universitario di Architettura
S. Croce 1957
30125 Venezia

# JAPAN – JAPON

HEAD OF DELEGATION

Ms. Junko Matsukawa (Presenter)
President
Laboratory for Innovations of Quality of
Life
Shibakouen-Annex
1-8 Shibakouen 3-chome
Minato-ku
Tokyo 105

OFFICIAL DELEGATION

Ms. Tomoko Okiyama
Urban Planning Section
Corporate Business Development
TOA Corporation
5 Yonbanchou Chiyodaku
Tokyo 102

Mr. Shunichi Kuwata
Housing Policy Division
Ministry of Construction
2-1-3 Kasumigaseki
Chiyoda-ku
Tokyo 100

Ms. Ayumi Rai
Section Chief
Housing Policy Division
Housing Bureau
Ministry of Construction
2-1-3 Kasumigaseki
Chiyoda-ku
Tokyo 100

Ms. Hatsue Tamura
Director for Improvement
of Environment for Child-Care
Cildren and Families Division
Bureau of Social Welfare
Tokyo Metropolitan Government
Nishi-shinjuku 2-8-1 Shinjuku-ku
Tokyo 163-01

PERMANENT DELEGATION
TO THE OECD

Mr. Hidekazu Ingawa
First Secretary

Mr. Mitsuo Sakaba
Counsellor

Ms. Mana Kumekawa
Technical Assistant

# MEXICO – MEXIQUE

HEAD OF DELEGATION

OFFICIAL DELEGATION

OTHER PARTICIPANTS

Ms. Ruth Hernandez Martinez
Attorney at Law
Regidora
XIV Ayuntamiento de Tijuana
City of Tijuana
Av. Independencia y Paseo Tijuana
Zona Urbana Rio Tijuana
Tijuana, Baja California 22320

# THE NETHERLANDS – PAYS-BAS

OFFICIAL DELEGATION

Ms. Teresa Fogelberg
Head of Special Programme
Women and Development
Directorate General of International
Cooperation
Ministry of Foreign Affairs
P.O. Box 20061
2500 EB The Hague

Dr. Antoinette H. Gosses
Senior Adviser Women and Development
Directorate General of International
Cooperation
Ministry of Foreign Affairs
P.O. Box 20061
2500 EB The Hague

Ms. Caroline Herlaar
Ministry of Social Affairs and Employment
Department for the Co-ordination of
Emancipation Policy (DCE)
P.O. Box 90801
2509 GV The Hague

Ms. Ettjen Modderman
Senior Research Officer
National Spatial Planning Agency
Ministry of Housing, Spatial Planning and
Environment
P.O. Box 30940
2500 GX Den Haag

Ms. Evelien Van Hercules
Traffic and Transport Affairs
National Spatial Planning Agency
Rijnstraat 2
P.O. Box 30940
2500 GX Den Haag

# NEW ZEALAND – NOUVELLE-ZÉLANDE

**HEAD OF DELEGATION**

Ms. Elizabeth Rowe
Chief Executive Officer
Ministry of Women's Affairs
Wellington

**OFFICIAL DELEGATION**

**OTHER PARTICIPANTS**

Ms. Patricia M. Austin
Lecturer
Department of Planning
Faculty of Architecture Property
and Planning
The University of Auckland
Auckland

# NORWAY – NORVÈGE

**HEAD OF DELEGATION**

Ms. Unni Mathisen (Presenter)
Political Adviser
Ministry of Environment
P.O. Box 8013 DEP
0030 Oslo 1

**OFFICIAL DELEGATION**

Ms. Kari Husabø (Presenter)
Assistant Director General
Ministry of Environment
P.O. Box 8013 DEP
0030 Oslo 1

Ms. Anne Margrethe Kaltenborn Lunde
Advisor
The Housing and Building Department
The Ministry of Local Government and
Labour
P.O. Box 8112 Oslo

Ms. Randi Skjerven (Presenter)
Project Co-ordinator
Ministry of Environment
P.O. Box 8013 DEP
0030 Oslo 1

**OTHER PARTICIPANTS**

Ms. Laila Aanerød
Norland Fylkeskommone
Fylkeshuset
Bodø 8002

Ms. Astrid Bonesmø
Adviser
Ministry of Environment
Boks 8013, Dep
N-0030 Oslo

# PORTUGAL

**HEAD OF DELEGATION**

Mme Helena Vaz da Silva (Chair of Session
on Women in Urban Planning)
Member of European Parliament
Centro Nacional de Cultura
Rua Antonio Maria Cardoso n° 68
P-1200 Lisbonne

**OFFICIAL DELEGATION**

Mme Maria de Lurdes Poeira (Rapporteur/
Member-Group on Urban Affairs)
Expert ( )
Direction générale de l'aménagement

du territoire
Rua Campo Grande, no. 50
1700 Lisbonne

**PERMANENT DELEGATION
TO THE OECD**

M. José A. da Silveira Godhino
Ambassadeur
OCDE Délégation Permanent

M. Luís Barros
Conseiller

# SWEDEN – SUÈDE

## HEAD OF DELEGATION

Ms. Mona Danielson
Assistant Under-Secretary
Ministry of Health and Social Affairs
S-103 33 Stockholm

## OFFICIAL DELEGATION

Mr. Lars Berggrund
Senior Comprehensive Planner
City Planning Authority
Box 2554
S-403 17 Göteborg

Ms. Lena Dübeck
Head of Section
Ministry of the Environment
and Natural Resources
S-103 33 Stockholm

Ms. Elizebeth Falemo
Political Adviser
Ministry of the Environment and natural
Resources
S-103 33 Stockholm

Ms. Lisbeth Fall
Chief Architect of the County
Administration
Länsstyrelsen i Jönköpings län
S-551 86 Jönköping

Ms. Tora Friberg Ph. D.
Department of Human and
Economic Geography
University of Lund
Sölvegatan 13
S-223 62 Lund

Ms. Sigrun Kaul
Professor
Nordic Institute for Studies
in Urban and Regional Planning
Box 1658
S-111 86 Stockholm

Dr. Annika von Scheele
Ph.D. Achitect
Doctor of Technology and
Chairwoman for
Women's Building Forum in Sweden
University of Örebro
Centre for Urban Research
Hagastrand 14
S-703 40 Örebro

## OTHER PARTICIPANTS

Ms. Marianne Bull
Researcher
National Rural Area Development Authority
Erik Dahlbergsgatan 12
Gothenburg
S-411 26

Dr. Cecilia Jensfelt
Assistant Professor
Snäckvägen 11
16136 Bromma

# SWITZERLAND – SUISSE

## HEAD OF DELEGATION

Mme Yvette Jaggi
Syndique de la ville de Lausanne
Hôtel de Ville
Case postale 3280
1002 Lausanne

## OFFICIAL DELEGATION

Mme Marianne Frischknecht
Directrice du Bureau de l'égalité
du Canton de Genève
2, rue de la Tannerie
1208 Carouge

Ms. Suzanne Michel (Presenter)
Brüggbühlstr. 46A
3172 Niederwangen

Lilli Monteventi (Presenter)
Communauté d'études pour
l'aménagement du territoire (C.E.A.T)
14, avenue de l'Église-Anglaise
1001 Lausanne

Ms. Agnès Rochat
Chargé de mission
Hôtel de Ville
Case postale 3280
1002 Lausanne

Ms. Doris Star
Communauté d'études pour
l'aménagement du territoire (C.E.A.T)
14, avenue de l'Église-Anglaise
1001 Lausanne

OTHER PARTICIPANTS

Mme Sylvie Cristina-Reichlin
Géographe/Présidente
Centre de documentation sur
la condition féminine et l'égalité
23, rue Louis-Favre
1201 Genève

Ms. Françoise Lieberherr
Développement équilibré hommes-femmes
Direction de la coopération
au développement
et de l'aide humanitaire (DDA)
Eigerstr. 73
CH-3003 Berne

## TURKEY – TURQUIE

HEAD OF DELEGATION

Mrs. Yildiz Tokman
Head of Division
Prime Ministry Housing Development
Administration
Ankara

OFFICIAL DELEGATION

Ms. Gülfer Cezayirli
Urban Planner and Architect
Ministry of Public Works and Settlement
Necatibey Cad. No. 63
Ankara

PERMANENT DELEGATION
TO THE OECD

Mr. Ipar Önel
Deputy Economic and Commercial
Counsellor

## UNITED KINGDOM – ROYAUME-UNI

HEAD OF DELEGATION

Mr. John Zetter
(Chairman-Group on Urban Affairs)
Head
International Planning Division
Department of the Environment
2 Marsham St.
London SW1 3EB

OFFICIAL DELEGATION

Ms. Jo Beall (Presenter)
London School of Economics and Political
Science
Houghton Street
London WC2A 2AE

Ms. Domini Gunn-Peim (Presenter)
Area Manager
Renewal and Grants
Housing Department
City of Leicester
35 Rowsley Street
Leicester LE5 5JP

Professor Patsy Healey (Presenter)
Director
Centre for Research in European Environ-
ments
Claremont Tower
University of Newcastle upon Tyne
Newcastle upon Tyne NE1 7RU

Ms. Sue Laughlin (Presenter)
Chairperson
Women's Health Working Group
Glasgow Healthy Cities Project
Greater Glasgow Health Board
231 George Street
Glasgow G2 2UR

Dr. Gillian McIlwaine (Presenter)
Consultant in Public Health
Greater Glasgow Health Board
Glasgow Royal Maternity Hospital
Rottenrow
Glasgow G4 0NA

Dr. Sule Takmaz Nisancioglu (Presenter)
Team Leader
Environment Policy Team
Planning Department
Barnet Council
London N20 0EJ

Professor Elizabeth Wilson (Presenter)
School of Information and Communication
Studies
Faculty of Environmental and Social Studies
University of North London
Ladbroke House
62-66 Highbury Grove
London N5 2AD

OTHER PARTICIPANTS

Ms. Anne Branson (Presenter)
Assistant Director of Housing
Leicester City Council
35 Rowsley Street
Leicester LE5 5JP

Ms. Eve Brook
Chair of the Social Services Committee
Social Services Department
Birmingham City Council
C/o Yvonne Ashford,
Louisa Ryland House
44 Newhall Street
Birmingham B3 3PL

Ms. Linda Davies
Senior Lecturer
School of Town and Country Planning
Faculty of the Built Environment
University of the West of England
Coldharbour Lane
Bristol BS16 1QY

Ms. Sharon Fleming
Assistant Operations Manager
The Housing Corporation
Head Office
Maple House
149 Tottenham Court Road
London W1P 0BN

Ms. Dilys Fletcher
Chair
Higginshaw Village Estate
Management Board
37 Wimpole Street
Oldham OL1 3JN

Dr. Catherine Garner
Head of Innovation Services
Scottish Homes
Roseberry House
9 Haymarket Terrace
Edinburgh EH12 5YA

Ms. Clara Greed
Senior Lecturer
School of Planning
Faculty of the Built Environment
University of the West of England
Frenchay Campus
Coldharbour Lane
Bristol BS16 1QY

Ms. Caroline Heijne
Director
Women's Design Service
Johnson's Yard 2nd. Floor
4 Pinchin Street
London E1 1SA

Ms. Margaretha Holmstedt
European Briefing Unit
University of Bradford
Bradford BD71 DP

Ms. Helen Kay
Research Fellow
Centre for Housing Research and Urban
Studies
University of Glasgow
25 Bute Gardens
University of Glasgow
Glasgow G12 8RS

Ms. Catherine McKenzie
Researcher
Department of Geography
Lancaster University
Lancaster LA1 2TT

Cllr. Margaret Nolan
Trustee
Meadow Well Community Development
Trust
29 Newlyn Cres.
North Shields Tyne and Wear
North Shields NE29 7QN

Ms. Hina Popat
National Federation of Housing Associations
Regional Office for the East Midlands
3rd. Floor
The Rutland Centre
56 Halford Street
Leicester LE1 1TQ

Ms. Margaret A. Scott
Principal
Employment Policy, Urban Issues
Department of Employment HQ
Room 517 Caxton House
Tothill Street
London SW1H 9NF

Ms. Jane Smith
Housing Finance and Development
National Federation of Housing Associations
174 Gray's Inn Road
London WC1X 8UP

Ms. Eleanor Taylor
Head of Equal Opportunities
Scottish Enterprise
120 Bothwell Street
Glasgow G2 YJP

Ms. Janet Williams
Acting Executive Support Officer
Policy Unit
Urban Renewal Division
Environmental Services Department
Birmingham City Council
67 Curzon Street
Birmingham B4 7DH

Ms. Gillian Young
Research Manager
Scottish Homes
Roseberry House
9 Haymarket Terrace
Edinburgh EH12 5YA

## UNITED STATES – ÉTATS-UNIS

HEAD OF DELEGATION

OFFICIAL DELEGATION

OTHER PARTICIPANTS

Mr. Michael Brinda (Presenter)
Minnesota Center for Community
Economic Development
Room 331 City Hall
350 Fifth-St.-Sth.
Minneapolis
MN 55415

Dr. Nancy Diamond
Environment Adviser
USAID
Office of Women and Development
SA-18, Room 714
20523-1816 Washington D.C.

Ms. Sandy Schilen (Presenter)
Neighbourhood Women's Renaissance Board
New York

# COMMISSION OF THE EUROPEAN COMMUNITIES

Dr. Marina Alberti
Expert Consultant
EEA - TTF DG XI
Commission européenne
Bd. du Triomphe 174
B 1169 Bruxelles
BELGIUM

Mr. Eric den Hamer
DG XI
European Commission
200, rue de la Loi
B 1049 Bruxelles
BELGIUM

Ms. Nedialka Sougareva
Groupe d'experts sur
l'environnement urbain
Commission européenne DG XI
Ministère de l'Environnement
Direction nature et paysages
20, avenue de Ségur
75007 Paris
FRANCE

Ms. Maria Stratigaki
Experte
Unité pour l'égalité des femmes
et des hommes
Commission européenne DG V. A.3
200, rue de la Loi
B 1049 Bruxelles
BELGIUM

## NON-MEMBER COUNTRIES
## ALBANIA – ALBANIE

Ms. Tatjana Harito MD
Director
Department of Public Health
Ministry of Health
Tirana

## KAZAKHSTAN

Mme Jeanette Jarmagambetova
Docteur ès Sciences Techniques
Vice-Recteur
Institut Technologique d'Almaty
Appt. 7, 17 rue Baribaïéva
480002 Almaty

## POLAND – POLOGNE

Dr. Hanna Wieczorek
Director of the Department of Public Health
Municipal Office of Lodz
Sienkiewicza 5
Lodz 90 - 113

## RUSSIA – RUSSIE

Ms. Shubina Vladimirovna
Vice Chair
Committee on Social Affairs
Mayors Office,-St.-Petersburg
193 060 St. Petersburg, Smolny

Professor Lidia Simbirtseva
Co-ordinator
Women's Health in-St.-Petersburg
Head of Department-Healthy Lifestyles
International Institute of Women
and Management
Pinski per. 7-26
195 009 St. Petersburg

## TAJIKISTAN – TADJIKISTAN

Ms. Eugenia Narzulaeva
Institute of Obs/Gyn and
Paediatrics
Tursun-sade 31
Dushanbe 734002

## INTERNATIONAL ORGANISATIONS

COUNCIL OF EUROPE
Ms. Christiana Storelli
Council of Europe
Via C. Ghringhelli 5
CH-6500 Bellinzona
SWITZERLAND

EUROPEAN FOUNDATION
FOR THE IMPROVEMENT OF LIVING
AND WORKING CONDITIONS
Mr. Jørn Pedersen
Co-ordinator
Environment Programme
European Foundation for the Improvement
of Living and Working Conditions
Loughlinstown House
Shankhill
Co. Dublin
IRELAND

UNCHS (Habitat)

Ms. Catalina Hinchey Trujillo (Presenter)
Co-ordinator
Women in Human Settlements
Development Programme
UNCHS (Habitat)
P.O. Box 30030
Nairobi
KENYA

UNECE

Ms. Christina von Schweinichen (Presenter)
Human Settlements Section
United Nations Economic Commission
for Europe
Palais des Nations
CH-1211 Genèva
SWITZERLAND

# OECD

**Secrétariat**
Mr. Staffan Sohlman
Secretary General

M. Pierre Vinde
Deputy Secretary General

Office of the Secretary General
M. Philippe Montigny

**Territorial Development Service**
Mr. Chris Brooks
Director

**Urban Affairs Division**
Mr. Ariel Alexandre
Head

Mr. Josef Konvitz
Principal Administrator

Ms. Lindsay MacFarlane
(Conference Secretariat)
Administrator

Mr. Richard Ebbs (Conference Secretariat)
Consultant

Mr. Nicola De Michelis
Consultant

Mr. Atsushi Ichikawa
Trainee

**Local Economic and Employment
Development Programme
(LEED Programme)**
Mr. Sergio Arzeni
Head

Ms. Genevieve Lecamp
Administrator

**Environment Directorate**
Ms. Eva Rosinger
Deputy Director

**Directorate for Development Cooperation**
Ms. Francesca Cook
Administrator

**Directorate for Education, Employment,
Labour and Social Affairs**

**Role of women in the Economy**
Ms. Françoise Coré
Administrator

**OECD Observer**
Ms. Ulla Ranhall-Reyners
Editor

# MAIN SALES OUTLETS OF OECD PUBLICATIONS
# PRINCIPAUX POINTS DE VENTE DES PUBLICATIONS DE L'OCDE

**ARGENTINA – ARGENTINE**
Carlos Hirsch S.R.L.
Galería Güemes, Florida 165, 4° Piso
1333 Buenos Aires    Tel. (1) 331.1787 y 331.2391
                     Telefax: (1) 331.1787

**AUSTRALIA – AUSTRALIE**
D.A. Information Services
648 Whitehorse Road, P.O.B 163
Mitcham, Victoria 3132    Tel. (03) 873.4411
                          Telefax: (03) 873.5679

**AUSTRIA – AUTRICHE**
Gerold & Co.
Graben 31
Wien I    Tel. (0222) 533.50.14
          Telefax: (0222) 512.47.31.29

**BELGIUM – BELGIQUE**
Jean De Lannoy
Avenue du Roi 202 Koningslaan
B-1060 Bruxelles    Tel. (02) 538.51.69/538.08.41
                    Telefax: (02) 538.08.41

**CANADA**
Renouf Publishing Company Ltd.
1294 Algoma Road
Ottawa, ON K1B 3W8    Tel. (613) 741.4333
                      Telefax: (613) 741.5439
Stores:
61 Sparks Street
Ottawa, ON K1P 5R1    Tel. (613) 238.8985
211 Yonge Street
Toronto, ON M5B 1M4    Tel. (416) 363.3171
                       Telefax: (416)363.59.63

Les Éditions La Liberté Inc.
3020 Chemin Sainte-Foy
Sainte-Foy, PQ G1X 3V6    Tel. (418) 658.3763
                          Telefax: (418) 658.3763

Federal Publications Inc.
165 University Avenue, Suite 701
Toronto, ON M5H 3B8    Tel. (416) 860.1611
                       Telefax: (416) 860.1608

Les Publications Fédérales
1185 Université
Montréal, QC H3B 3A7    Tel. (514) 954.1633
                        Telefax: (514) 954.1635

**CHINA – CHINE**
China National Publications Import
Export Corporation (CNPIEC)
16 Gongti E. Road, Chaoyang District
P.O. Box 88 or 50
Beijing 100704 PR    Tel. (01) 506.6688
                     Telefax: (01) 506.3101

**CHINESE TAIPEI – TAIPEI CHINOIS**
Good Faith Worldwide Int'l. Co. Ltd.
9th Floor, No. 118, Sec. 2
Chung Hsiao E. Road
Taipei    Tel. (02) 391.7396/391.7397
          Telefax: (02) 394.9176

**CZECH REPUBLIC – RÉPUBLIQUE TCHÈQUE**
Artia Pegas Press Ltd.
Narodni Trida 25
POB 825
111 21 Praha 1    Tel. 26.65.68
                  Telefax: 26.20.81

**DENMARK – DANEMARK**
Munksgaard Book and Subscription Service
35, Nørre Søgade, P.O. Box 2148
DK-1016 København K    Tel. (33) 12.85.70
                       Telefax: (33) 12.93.87

**EGYPT – ÉGYPTE**
Middle East Observer
41 Sherif Street
Cairo    Tel. 392.6919
         Telefax: 360-6804

**FINLAND – FINLANDE**
Akateeminen Kirjakauppa
Keskuskatu 1, P.O. Box 128
00100 Helsinki
Subscription Services/Agence d'abonnements :
P.O. Box 23
00371 Helsinki    Tel. (358 0) 121 4416
                  Telefax: (358 0) 121.4450

**FRANCE**
OECD/OCDE
Mail Orders/Commandes par correspondance:
2, rue André-Pascal
75775 Paris Cedex 16    Tel. (33-1) 45.24.82.00
                        Telefax: (33-1) 49.10.42.76
                        Telex: 640048 OCDE
Internet: Compte.PUBSINQ @ oecd.org
Orders via Minitel, France only/
Commandes par Minitel, France exclusivement :
36 15 OCDE

OECD Bookshop/Librairie de l'OCDE :
33, rue Octave-Feuillet
75016 Paris    Tel. (33-1) 45.24.81.81
               (33-1) 45.24.81.67

Documentation Française
29, quai Voltaire
75007 Paris    Tel. 40.15.70.00

Gibert Jeune (Droit-Économie)
6, place Saint-Michel
75006 Paris    Tel. 43.25.91.19

Librairie du Commerce International
10, avenue d'Iéna
75016 Paris    Tel. 40.73.34.60

Librairie Dunod
Université Paris-Dauphine
Place du Maréchal de Lattre de Tassigny
75016 Paris    Tel. (1) 44.05.40.13

Librairie Lavoisier
11, rue Lavoisier
75008 Paris    Tel. 42.65.39.95

Librairie L.G.D.J. - Montchrestien
20, rue Soufflot
75005 Paris    Tel. 46.33.89.85

Librairie des Sciences Politiques
30, rue Saint-Guillaume
75007 Paris    Tel. 45.48.36.02

P.U.F.
49, boulevard Saint-Michel
75005 Paris    Tel. 43.25.83.40

Librairie de l'Université
12a, rue Nazareth
13100 Aix-en-Provence    Tel. (16) 42.26.18.08

Documentation Française
165, rue Garibaldi
69003 Lyon    Tel. (16) 78.63.32.23

Librairie Decitre
29, place Bellecour
69002 Lyon    Tel. (16) 72.40.54.54

Librairie Sauramps
Le Triangle
34967 Montpellier Cedex 2    Tel. (16) 67.58.85.15
                             Tekefax: (16) 67.58.27.36

**GERMANY – ALLEMAGNE**
OECD Publications and Information Centre
August-Bebel-Allee 6
D-53175 Bonn    Tel. (0228) 959.120
                Telefax: (0228) 959.12.17

**GREECE – GRÈCE**
Librairie Kauffmann
Mavrokordatou 9
106 78 Athens    Tel. (01) 32.55.321
                 Telefax: (01) 32.30.320

**HONG-KONG**
Swindon Book Co. Ltd.
Astoria Bldg. 3F
34 Ashley Road, Tsimshatsui
Kowloon, Hong Kong    Tel. 2376.2062
                      Telefax: 2376.0685

**HUNGARY – HONGRIE**
Euro Info Service
Margitsziget, Európa Ház
1138 Budapest    Tel. (1) 111.62.16
                 Telefax: (1) 111.60.61

**ICELAND – ISLANDE**
Mál Mog Menning
Laugavegi 18, Pósthólf 392
121 Reykjavik    Tel. (1) 552.4240
                 Telefax: (1) 562.3523

**INDIA – INDE**
Oxford Book and Stationery Co.
Scindia House
New Delhi 110001    Tel. (11) 331.5896/5308
                    Telefax: (11) 332.5993
17 Park Street
Calcutta 700016    Tel. 240832

**INDONESIA – INDONÉSIE**
Pdii-Lipi
P.O. Box 4298
Jakarta 12042    Tel. (21) 573.34.67
                 Telefax: (21) 573.34.67

**IRELAND – IRLANDE**
Government Supplies Agency
Publications Section
4/5 Harcourt Road
Dublin 2    Tel. 661.31.11
            Telefax: 475.27.60

**ISRAEL**
Praedicta
5 Shatner Street
P.O. Box 34030
Jerusalem 91430    Tel. (2) 52.84.90/1/2
                   Telefax: (2) 52.84.93

R.O.Y. International
P.O. Box 13056
Tel Aviv 61130    Tel. (3) 546 1423
                  Telefax: (3) 546 1442

Palestinian Authority/Middle East:
INDEX Information Services
P.O.B. 19502
Jerusalem    Tel. (2) 27.12.19
             Telefax: (2) 27.16.34

**ITALY – ITALIE**
Libreria Commissionaria Sansoni
Via Duca di Calabria 1/1
50125 Firenze    Tel. (055) 64.54.15
                 Telefax: (055) 64.12.57
Via Bartolini 29
20155 Milano    Tel. (02) 36.50.83
Editrice e Libreria Herder
Piazza Montecitorio 120
00186 Roma    Tel. 679.46.28
              Telefax: 678.47.51
Libreria Hoepli
Via Hoepli 5
20121 Milano    Tel. (02) 86.54.46
                Telefax: (02) 805.28.86
Libreria Scientifica
Dott. Lucio de Biasio 'Aeiou'
Via Coronelli, 6
20146 Milano    Tel. (02) 48.95.45.52
                Telefax: (02) 48.95.45.48

**JAPAN – JAPON**
OECD Publications and Information Centre
Landic Akasaka Building
2-3-4 Akasaka, Minato-ku
Tokyo 107    Tel. (81.3) 3586.2016
             Telefax: (81.3) 3584.7929

**KOREA – CORÉE**
Kyobo Book Centre Co. Ltd.
P.O. Box 1658, Kwang Hwa Moon
Seoul    Tel. 730.78.91
         Telefax: 735.00.30

**MALAYSIA – MALAISIE**
University of Malaya Bookshop
University of Malaya
P.O. Box 1127, Jalan Pantai Baru
59700 Kuala Lumpur
Malaysia                    Tel. 756.5000/756.5425
                            Telefax: 756.3246

**MEXICO – MEXIQUE**
Revistas y Periodicos Internacionales S.A. de C.V.
Florencia 57 - 1004
Mexico, D.F. 06600          Tel. 207.81.00
                            Telefax: 208.39.79

**NETHERLANDS – PAYS-BAS**
SDU Uitgeverij Plantijnstraat
Externe Fondsen
Postbus 20014
2500 EA's-Gravenhage        Tel. (070) 37.89.880
Voor bestellingen:     Telefax: (070) 34.75.778

**NEW ZEALAND
NOUVELLE-ZÉLANDE**
GPLegislation Services
P.O. Box 12418
Thorndon, Wellington        Tel. (04) 496.5655
                            Telefax: (04) 496.5698

**NORWAY – NORVÈGE**
Narvesen Info Center – NIC
Bertrand Narvesens vei 2
P.O. Box 6125 Etterstad
0602 Oslo 6                 Tel. (022) 57.33.00
                            Telefax: (022) 68.19.01

**PAKISTAN**
Mirza Book Agency
65 Shahrah Quaid-E-Azam
Lahore 54000                Tel. (42) 353.601
                            Telefax: (42) 231.730

**PHILIPPINE – PHILIPPINES**
International Book Center
5th Floor, Filipinas Life Bldg.
Ayala Avenue
Metro Manila                Tel. 81.96.76
                            Telex 23312 RHP PH

**PORTUGAL**
Livraria Portugal
Rua do Carmo 70-74
Apart. 2681
1200 Lisboa                 Tel. (01) 347.49.82/5
                            Telefax: (01) 347.02.64

**SINGAPORE – SINGAPOUR**
Gower Asia Pacific Pte Ltd.
Golden Wheel Building
41, Kallang Pudding Road, No. 04-03
Singapore 1334              Tel. 741.5166
                            Telefax: 742.9356

**SPAIN – ESPAGNE**
Mundi-Prensa Libros S.A.
Castelló 37, Apartado 1223
Madrid 28001                Tel. (91) 431.33.99
                            Telefax: (91) 575.39.98

Libreria Internacional AEDOS
Consejo de Ciento 391
08009 – Barcelona           Tel. (93) 488.30.09
                            Telefax: (93) 487.76.59

Llibreria de la Generalitat
Palau Moja
Rambla dels Estudis, 118
08002 – Barcelona
            (Subscripcions) Tel. (93) 318.80.12
            (Publicacions) Tel. (93) 302.67.23
                            Telefax: (93) 412.18.54

**SRI LANKA**
Centre for Policy Research
c/o Colombo Agencies Ltd.
No. 300-304, Galle Road
Colombo 3              Tel. (1) 574240, 573551-2
                       Telefax: (1) 575394, 510711

**SWEDEN – SUÈDE**
Fritzes Customer Service
S–106 47 Stockholm          Tel. (08) 690.90.90
                            Telefax: (08) 20.50.21

Subscription Agency/Agence d'abonnements :
Wennergren-Williams Info AB
P.O. Box 1305
171 25 Solna                Tel. (08) 705.97.50
                            Telefax: (08) 27.00.71

**SWITZERLAND – SUISSE**
Maditec S.A. (Books and Periodicals - Livres
et périodiques)
Chemin des Palettes 4
Case postale 266
1020 Renens VD 1            Tel. (021) 635.08.65
                            Telefax: (021) 635.07.80

Librairie Payot S.A.
4, place Pépinet
CP 3212
1002 Lausanne               Tel. (021) 341.33.47
                            Telefax: (021) 341.33.45

Librairie Unilivres
6, rue de Candolle
1205 Genève                 Tel. (022) 320.26.23
                            Telefax: (022) 329.73.18

Subscription Agency/Agence d'abonnements :
Dynapresse Marketing S.A.
38 avenue Vibert
1227 Carouge                Tel. (022) 308.07.89
                            Telefax: (022) 308.07.99

See also – Voir aussi :
OECD Publications and Information Centre
August-Bebel-Allee 6
D-53175 Bonn (Germany)      Tel. (0228) 959.120
                            Telefax: (0228) 959.12.17

**THAILAND – THAÏLANDE**
Suksit Siam Co. Ltd.
113, 115 Fuang Nakhon Rd.
Opp. Wat Rajbopith
Bangkok 10200               Tel. (662) 225.9531/2
                            Telefax: (662) 222.5188

**TURKEY – TURQUIE**
Kültür Yayinlari Is-Türk Ltd. Sti.
Atatürk Bulvari No. 191/Kat 13
Kavaklidere/Ankara    Tel. 428.11.40 Ext. 2458
Dolmabahce Cad. No. 29
Besiktas/Istanbul           Tel. (312) 260 7188
                            Telex: (312) 418 29 46

**UNITED KINGDOM – ROYAUME-UNI**
HMSO
Gen. enquiries              Tel. (171) 873 8496
Postal orders only:
P.O. Box 276, London SW8 5DT
Personal Callers HMSO Bookshop
49 High Holborn, London WC1V 6HB
                            Telefax: (171) 873 8416
Branches at: Belfast, Birmingham, Bristol,
Edinburgh, Manchester

**UNITED STATES – ÉTATS-UNIS**
OECD Publications and Information Center
2001 L Street N.W., Suite 650
Washington, D.C. 20036-4910 Tel. (202) 785.6323
                            Telefax: (202) 785.0350

**VENEZUELA**
Libreria del Este
Avda F. Miranda 52, Aptdo. 60337
Edificio Galipán
Caracas 106   Tel. 951.1705/951.2307/951.1297
                        Telegram: Libreste Caracas

Subscription to OECD periodicals may also be
placed through main subscription agencies.

Les abonnements aux publications périodiques de
l'OCDE peuvent être souscrits auprès des
principales agences d'abonnement.

Orders and inquiries from countries where Distribu-
tors have not yet been appointed should be sent to:
OECD Publications Service, 2 rue André-Pascal,
75775 Paris Cedex 16, France.

Les commandes provenant de pays où l'OCDE n'a
pas encore désigné de distributeur peuvent être
adressées à : OCDE, Service des Publications,
2, rue André-Pascal, 75775 Paris Cedex 16, France.

7-1995